Palgrave Studies in Equity, Diversity, Inclusion, and Indigenization in Business

Series Editor
Eddy S. Ng, Queen's University, Kingston, ON, Canada

This series seeks to assemble scholarly research around equity, diversity, inclusion, and indigenization in the business world. The books in this series will explore contemporary diversity topics such as gender and corporate governance, sexuality and career development, social justice in the workplace, race and marketing, Indigenous inclusion, supplier diversity, mental health and neurodiversity at work, and more.

Through rigorous, disciplinary and interdisciplinary research and contributions from leading scholars, this series will provide an in-depth exploration of each topic and challenge scholars and practitioners to consider expanding their own awareness while addressing ways to make business (and society) more inclusive. The series speaks on behalf of anyone who has ever been affected–directly or indirectly–by discrimination or exclusion.

Ed Hasan

Embracing Workplace Religious Diversity and Inclusion

Key Challenges and Solutions

Ed Hasan
Georgetown University
Washington, DC, USA

ISSN 2731-7307   ISSN 2731-7315 (electronic)
Palgrave Studies in Equity, Diversity, Inclusion, and Indigenization in Business
ISBN 978-3-030-89772-7   ISBN 978-3-030-89773-4 (eBook)
https://doi.org/10.1007/978-3-030-89773-4

Cover illustration: Maram shutterstock.com

This Palgrave Macmillan imprint is published by the registered company Springer Nature Switzerland AG
The registered company address is: Gewerbestrasse 11, 6330 Cham, Switzerland

I dedicate this book to my wife and children. My wife's real-life workplace experiences inspired me to write this book. She motivated me to embark on this journey, and she kept me going even during the most challenging times. Rana, you are my best friend, my backbone, and my world. You've made me a better husband, father, and person. It was your love, encouragement, and support that helped me accomplish this. To my children—who served as a reminder of what is truly important in life—thank you for your hugs, kisses, and smiles that made this process so much easier for me. I hope this book will motivate you to do something bigger and better for the world.

FOREWORD

This book is very important because religious literacy is important. I don't mean a deep knowledge of various religious beliefs and practices; rather, it is knowledge about how religion impacts the workplace and the marketplace, our coworkers, and partners as well as our customers and clients. The data Ed Hasan presents throughout the book are extremely helpful. A few key statistics are worth highlighting.

First, religion is not in decline. As my colleagues and I demonstrated, our planet is projected to have 2.3 billion more religiously affiliated people by 2050 compared with just 0.1 billion more religiously unaffiliated people (Hackett et al., 2015). That's like religion "winning" 23-to-1.

This religious growth is also changing the global marketplace. Today, three of the top five economies are Christian majority. But in 40 years, only one is projected to be. The other four top economies in 2050 will include countries where Hindus, Muslims, Buddhists, and the unaffiliated predominate (Grim & Connor, 2015). And, as we showed, while Muslim populations are growing the fastest, the greatest gains in the share of the global GDP are projected to be among Hindu populations. Companies that are religiously literate about these two global faiths have an advantage, and workplaces that are consciously accommodating to Muslims and Hindus will be able to tap into the innovative talent coming from these communities.

Indeed, research shows that this religious growth and diversity can be good for the workplace and the bottom lines of businesses as long as they are accompanied by respect for freedom of religion or belief (Grim et al., 2014). In such marketplaces and societies, innovative strength is more than twice as high as in societies that don't respect freedom of religion or belief. So, freedom to believe—or not believe—is good for business.

However, since 2009, the number of people living in countries with high religious restrictions and hostilities has increased from 4.8 to 5.9 billion people; that's an increase of 1.1 billion more people living in countries where freedom of religion or belief is under duress, based on my analysis of studies from the Pew Research Center (2021). The same Pew studies show that social hostilities involving religion in the U.S. are high. One place we see this is in the number of American workers who have experienced or witnessed religious discrimination in their workplace.

A Tanenbaum survey (2013) finds that 36% of American workers, or about 50 million people, have experienced or witnessed some form of religious discrimination or non-accommodation in their workplace.

Despite this, religious diversity and inclusion are not on the minds of many companies. Companies have rightly paid a lot of attention to other diversity and inclusion issues, such as sexual orientation. Now, religion is the next big thing businesses need to pay attention to. In 2016, for instance, there were twice as many workplace discrimination complaints about religion as complaints about sexual orientation.

But there is also good news. We are starting to see significant movement in some of the world's biggest and most successful companies toward more faith-friendly, religiously accommodating workplaces (Grim & Johnson, 2022). It's been decades in the making for some, like Texas Instruments. For others, like Salesforce, it's new and rapidly growing. The Religious Freedom & Business Foundation's REDI Index (Religious Freedom & Business Foundation, 2022) https://religiousfre edomandbusiness.org/redi) finds this trend is propelled by company-sponsored faith-oriented employee resource groups and other programs. Google, Intel, American Express, and others score highly for supporting such initiatives. American Airlines does too. One of their Chief Flight Controllers is a priest and company chaplain. In fact, Tyson Foods has chaplains from various religions compassionately serving the needs of all employees regardless of faith or belief. Why do these companies do it? It's good for employees. It gives them a competitive advantage. And that's good for societies.

Ed Hasan's book fills a critical need by offering solutions and helping businesses become religiously literate. I believe that you will find it extremely useful, regardless of whether you are exploring this topic for the first time or are well-experienced and looking to deepen your commitment to including religion as part of your overall commitment to diversity, equity and inclusion.

Annapolis, MD, USA   Brian J. Grim, Ph.D.
                                        President, Religious Freedom &
                                            Business Foundation

REFERENCES

Grim, B. J., Clark, G., & Snyder, R. E. (2014). Is religious freedom good for business? A conceptual and empirical analysis. *Interdisciplinary Journal of Research on Religion, 10* (Article 4). https://www.religjournal.com/pdf/ijrr10004.pdf

Grim, B. J. & Connor, P. (2015). Changing religion, changing economies: Future global religious and economic growth. *Religious freedom & business foundation.* https://religiousfreedomandbusiness.org/changing-religion-and-changing-economies

Grim, B. J., & Johnson, K. (2022). Corporate religious diversity, equity and inclusion as covenantal pluralism. In C. Seiple & D. R. Hoover (Eds.), *The Routledge handbook of religious literacy, pluralism, and global engagement* (pp. 228–240). Routledge.

Hackett, C., Stonawski, M., Potančoková, M., Grim, B. J., & Skirbekk, V. (2015). The future size of religiously affiliated and unaffiliated populations. *Demographic Research, 32* (Article 2774). https://www.demographic-research.org/volumes/vol32/27/

Pew Research Center. (2021). *Religious freedom & restrictions.* https://www.pewresearch.org/topic/religion/religious-freedom-restrictions/

Religious Freedom & Business Foundation. (2022). *Corporate religious equity, diversity & inclusion (REDI) index.* https://religiousfreedomandbusiness.org/redi

Tanenbaum. (2013). *What American workers really think about religion.* https://tanenbaum.org/product/what-american-workers-really-think-about-religion-tanenbaums-2013-survey-of-american-workers-and-religion-2/

Acknowledgments

This book is a collaborative effort, formed by seen and unseen influences both on my life and on the manuscript itself. It began as a doctoral dissertation and evolved into the book you hold in your hands over many drafts with the concerted efforts of my own and others. I owe a debt of gratitude to not only the people who touched this manuscript and my own life, but also to those whose research helped form the information contained herein. (I genuinely hope you will read the works cited in this book to learn more about religious diversity and inclusion.)

In particular, I feel a deep sense of gratitude:

- To my colleague and friend, Dr. Ifedapo Adeleye, for your mentorship and guidance. This would not have been possible without you.
- To my professors and colleagues for their support while I was completing my doctoral program at the University of Southern California: Dr. Courtney Malloy, Dr. Omar Ezzeldine, Dr. Shafiqa Ahmadi, and Dr. Kimberly Hirabayashi.
- To Imam Mohamed Hag Magid, for encouraging individuals to participate in my dissertation survey.
- To my colleagues Dorian Zimmerman, Furo Bakare, Ebes Esho, and Chelsea Stearns for your input, guidance, and research throughout this process.

- To my colleagues and students at Georgetown University for their encouragement and support.
- To the Lauren Taylor Shute Editorial team, for their world-class editorial services.
- And, to S. E. Fleenor, Senior Editor, for keeping my creative juices flowing, and keeping the process in check.

CONTENTS

ABOUT THE AUTHOR

Dr. Ed Hasan a practicing Muslim, is Palestinian American. He is the CEO of Kaizen Human Capital, an evidence-based organizational development, coaching, and training firm. He is an Adjunct Professor at Georgetown University, and a Subject Matter Expert and Instructor for the Society for Human Resource Management. He is a frequent speaker on workplace diversity and inclusion, culture, and leadership. Dr. Ed was recognized as one of George Mason University's Prominent Patriots in Business, exemplifying his engagement as a well-rounded scholar and a person prepared to act through innovation. He was a recipient of Georgetown University's Outstanding Faculty Award, which recognized him as a consummate professor and a role model for inclusive excellence. Dr. Ed received a doctoral degree in education from the University of Southern California where his research focus was religious inclusion in the workplace.

ABBREVIATIONS

9/11	The September 11 Terror Attacks
ACLU	American Civil Liberties Union
ADL	Anti-Defamation League
CCMA	South African Commission for Conciliation, Mediation, and Arbitration
CEO	Chief Executive Officer
CERD	Convention on the Elimination of all forms of Racial Discrimination
CFO	Chief Financial Officer
CJEU	The Court of Justice of the European Union
COVID-19	Coronavirus Disease 2019
CRC	Convention of the Rights of the Child
C-Suite	High-ranking executive titles in an organization as in chief
EEOC	United States Equal Employment Opportunity Commission
ERG	Employee Resource Group
EU	European Union
HR	Human Resources
ICCPR	International Covenant on Civil and Political Rights
IDE	Inclusion, Diversity, and Equality
IT	Information Technology
Kaizen HC	Kaizen Human Capital
LGBTQ+	An acronym referring to Lesbian, Gay, Bisexual, Transgender, and Queer people, and others who may identify with this group
NGO	Non-Government Organizations
RFRA	Religious Freedom and Restoration Act of 1993
SOAR	Strengths, Opportunities, Aspirations, and Trends

STRIDE	The Met's Strategy for Inclusion, Diversity, and Engagement
The Met	The London Metropolitan Police Force
UK	United Kingdom
UN	United Nations
U.S.	United States

Hijabs, Crucifixes, and Yarmulkes: Defining and Understanding Religious Inclusion in the Workplace

CHAPTER 1

Introduction

Abstract Despite exaggerated reports of their decline, religious populations and religious diversity continue to grow around the world. It is therefore not surprising that religion is featured prominently in the political realm and gaining more attention in the workplace. However, religion remains one of the "forgotten" dimensions of diversity, with too many organizations choosing to avoid it in their inclusion initiatives. This introductory chapter documents the unacceptable outcomes of this avoidance—religious discrimination, identity covering, and exclusion. The case is made for the business values, moral authority, and legal requirements for religious diversity and inclusion in the workplace.

Keywords Religious diversity · Workplace stigma · Religious freedom and business · Religious anti-discrimination laws · Inclusive workplace culture

Aaron was denied employment in a fast-food restaurant chain because he refused to shave his beard to meet the clean-shaven look required by the corporate appearance policies; Aaron is Jewish and keeps his beard as an observance of his religion. Mariam, a Muslim woman who wears a head scarf, didn't receive an anticipated promotion in her organization because

E. Hasan, *Embracing Workplace Religious Diversity and Inclusion*, Palgrave Studies in Equity, Diversity, Inclusion, and Indigenization in Business, https://doi.org/10.1007/978-3-030-89773-4_1

3

the new position required interaction with the public and her employers feared that her hijab would upset customers. When Felix revealed that he was not of the same Christian denomination as most of his colleagues, he was mocked and ridiculed.

These vignettes are based on real-life workplace scenarios that have occurred in workplaces in the U.S. and around the world. Research conducted in the U.S. found that Muslim job seekers who stated their religious affiliation received fewer interview invitations from employers than applicants who listed no religion; a similar study found that job seekers who included belonging to student religious organizations on their resumes received fewer responses from employers than those who made no mention of religion (BBC, 2014). These, and many of the examples you'll read in this book, show that religious discrimination plays a role in the hiring process in the U.S. and beyond.

Unfavorable treatment of individuals at work because of their religious beliefs and practices is not limited to adherents of one religion. They are becoming regular experiences of individuals across many religions and geographies. Even individuals who do not adhere to any religion have been victims of religious discrimination in the workplace. A 2021 study found, for example, that atheists were more likely to be viewed as a threat in the workplace, and thus, more likely to have their religion-related requests at work denied (Rios et al., 2021).

Workplace religious discrimination comes in different forms, and can occur before, during, and after the process of employment at the workplace. Many cases of workplace religious discrimination stem from employers; others from fellow employees.

Unfortunately, conversations regarding workplace discrimination often focus narrowly on gender and race issues while religious diversity is neglected entirely, largely due to the dearth of information about how to approach workplace religious diversity and inclusion. We must give religious inclusion adequate attention to create a safer, better world of work for all employees, and to enhance individual and organizational performance. In pursuing this goal, some of the following questions arise:

- What exactly constitutes workplace religious discrimination?
- How can individuals protect themselves against potential religious discrimination that could arise in the workplace?
- What can organizations do to stem the rising tide of religious discrimination that is becoming more common in many workplaces?

• Perhaps, most importantly, how can organizations ensure that their employees feel a sense of belonging inclusive of their religious beliefs and practices?

These are the questions I address in this book, published as part of the Palgrave Studies in Equity, Diversity, Inclusion, and Indigenization in Business series. I will explore contemporary challenges posed by religion in the workplace and provide solutions from multiple perspectives. Notably, I will offer a model for evaluation that should be very helpful: The Kaizen HC Model of Religious Inclusion. Ultimately, my hope is that close examination of this topic will provoke thoughtful and meaningful conversations aimed at solving religious discrimination today and far into the future.

Why Does Workplace Religious Diversity, Inclusion, and Discrimination Matter?

Throughout this book, I will explore various dimensions of the prevalence and impact of religious diversity and inclusion, as well as religious discrimination, with a narrow focus on the workplace and the societal factors that influence religious discrimination workplace environments.

Religious bias and stigma in the workplace are a reflection of stereotyping and cultural tensions from the proximal society. This stigma creates divisions and inequalities, though sometimes invisible, can affect the welfare and well-being of workers (Nachmias & Caven, 2019). Consequently, employees may engage in "covering," a phenomenon whereby an employee hides personal attributes that have a feared potential to result in being stigmatized—and yet those employees may still suffer silently in the workplace. Tackling issues of stigma in the workplace should be paramount to any organization seeking to ensure inclusiveness within a diverse employee population.

Though religion exists as a central influence of personal identities it has become a forgotten dimension of workplace diversity. The following chapters will explore the global trends that are a huge driver of religious diversity. In the U.S. and other Western countries, for example, the discourse on workplace religious diversity and inclusion tends to be dominated by advocates of Christian rights fending off increasing secularization and the declining influence of Christianity in the workplace and society.

In these same countries, however, voices are heard protesting the stigma and bias that religious minorities (especially immigrants) face. For organizations seeking to embrace religious inclusion, therefore, attention must be paid to the challenges and issues facing both the religious outgroup and the ingroup.

BUSINESS, MORAL, AND LEGAL CASES FOR RELIGIOUS DIVERSITY AND INCLUSION

People are the most important resource of any organization. Besides the roles they perform, they are the source of ideas, creativity, innovation, and connectivity with each other, other organizations, customers, and external stakeholders. The knowledge, skills, and abilities of employees and workers define the bedrock of knowledge and capabilities of any organization. Generally, diversity unlocks innovation, drives growth (Hewlett et al., 2013), and increases productivity as employees bring together their knowledge and experiences from diverse backgrounds.

Excluding or even giving the appearance of exclusion of any group of employees or potential employees who profess their religious identity constitutes a major competitive disadvantage. Multinational organizations especially stand to benefit from having a religiously diverse workforce. The global marketplace increasingly requires businesses to interact with stakeholders based in countries with diverse religions and cultures. Religious diversity in the workplace is therefore a crucial asset as diverse views and alternative approaches to management can be harnessed to enhance organizational performance (Syed et al., 2017).

In many Western countries, the war for talent is increasingly being won by organizations that are seen to take diversity issues seriously. Religious job seekers may be more inclined to work for organizations that pay particular attention to religious diversity and inclusion. However, it is not enough to merely accommodate religious diversity, nor do benefits automatically arise from having a religiously diverse workforce. Deriving optimal benefits from a religiously diverse workforce requires proactive and effective management aware of the dangers of real or perceived conflicts and inequality associated with inclusion efforts.

The moral imperative for the proactive management of religious diversity in the workplace is twofold. First, respect for other people's religious beliefs and the fostering of religious understanding and inclusion in the workplace is a show of respect for the fundamental human right of every person to freedom of thought and freedom of religion, both of which are generally protected by legal statutes.

Second, almost all religions advocate for ethical and moral values such as integrity, honesty, self-discipline, kindness, and charity. Most organizations encourage, appreciate, and reward these attributes in their employees. Promoting and managing religious diversity presents avenues for organizations to access these noble attributes, principally through hiring people for whom these attributes are integral to their identity.

In addition to the business and moral cases for being inclusive of religion at work, in many countries managing religious diversity in the workplace has become a legal requirement. In Chapter 2, we explore the legal frameworks and cases for religious inclusion in depth.

The legal, business, and moral cases for workplace religious diversity and inclusion do not operate in isolation. They are interrelated and mutually reinforcing. The current legal provisions for religious freedom, for example, recognize the moral imperative to respect individuals' religious beliefs and practices. The moral case for organizations to actively manage religious diversity hinges on their obligation to adhere to legal provisions. These cases for religious inclusion also provide additional motivation for writing this book, as many people and organizations are largely unaware of contemporary issues relating to workplace religious diversity.

What to Expect from This Book

This book aims to provide a nuanced understanding of workplace religious diversity and inclusion. In Part I, workplace religious diversity and inclusion are defined and the subject of conceptual, theoretically-based, and empirical analyses. Part II explores various aspects and examples of workplace religious diversity and inclusion management, showcasing real-life examples of religion and spirituality in diverse workplace contexts in America, Asia, Europe, and Africa. These chapters are designed to provoke the contemplation of contemporary issues and challenges relating to workplace religious diversity from various religious perspectives.

Undeniably, workplaces are becoming more diverse. In the next chapter, we'll explore what religious diversity looks like, the historical and legal contexts of religious diversity, the definitions and debates of religious discrimination, and how inclusion is supported and thwarted by these factors.

REFERENCES

BBC. (2014). *Does religious bias begin with your CV?* https://www.bbc.com/worklife/article/20140730-reveal-religion-on-your-cv

Hewlett, S. A., Marshall, M., & Sherbin, L. (2013). How diversity can drive innovation. *Harvard Business Review.* https://hbr.org/2013/12/how-diversity-can-drive-innovation

Nachmias, S., & Caven, V. (2019). Inequality and organizational practice: Work and welfare. In S. Nachmias & V. Caven (Eds.), *Inequality and organizational practice, Volume 1: Work and welfare* (pp. 1–14). Palgrave Macmillan.

Rios, K., Halper, L. R., & Scheitle, C. P. (2021). Explaining anti-atheist discrimination in the workplace: The role of intergroup threat. *Psychology of Religion and Spirituality.* Advance online publication. https://doi.org/10.1037/rel0000326

Syed, J., Klarsfeld, A., Ngunjiri, F. W., & Härtel, C. (2017). Introduction: The complex interface of work and religion. In J. Syed, A. Klarsfeld, F. Wambura Ngunjiri, & C. Härtel (Eds.), *Religious diversity in the workplace* (pp. 1–5). Cambridge University Press.

CHAPTER 2

The Paradox of Workplace Religious Inclusion in Theory and in Practice

Abstract Because religious observance plays a role in society at large and in people's everyday lives, forward-thinking organizations need to embrace religious inclusion within their hiring practices. This chapter begins with a real-life story of a South African chef whose employer failed to grant an accommodation to undertake a traditional religious/healer training. The case highlights challenges in navigating diverse religious practices in the workplace, managing accommodation requests, and fostering a sense of belonging among employees. The chapter explores the complex intersections of religion and ethnicity/race, as well as legal frameworks shaping religious freedom, diversity, and inclusion around the world.

Keywords Religious expression · Religious discrimination · Diversity management · Workplace spirituality · South Africa

In early 2007 in Pretoria, South Africa, chef Johanna Mmoledi started to experience dizziness, headaches, visions, and dreams (News24, 2013). Mmoledi recognized the signs to be a state called *ukubiswa*, which signifies a calling to traditional healing in *ngoma*, an African indigenous religion. When she consulted a traditional healer, or *sangoma*, she was

© The Author(s), under exclusive license to Springer Nature Switzerland AG 2022
E. Hasan, *Embracing Workplace Religious Diversity and Inclusion*, Palgrave Studies in Equity, Diversity, Inclusion, and Indigenization in Business, https://doi.org/10.1007/978-3-030-89773-4_2

instructed to become a *sangoma* herself as a means of appeasing her ancestors.

Mmoledi embarked upon traditional healer training, apparently with the support of her employer who initially allowed her to work half-days so she could attend training in the afternoon. Mmoledi had worked for the same employer, Kievits Kroon estate, for eight years as a chef de partie for conferences and the estate's leisure programs. Nevertheless, when she requested a month of unpaid leave to complete her training, her employer declined to allow her the time off, offering instead to allow her one week's unpaid leave.

The final phase of Mmoledi's healer training required attending intense and deeply taxing rituals and ceremonies, and she presented her employer with a note from her *sangoma* that she needed to take a month off to complete her training due to her illness and premonitions. Mmoledi felt strongly that her mental state would decline if she didn't complete the training her religion and ancestors required of her. Her employer deemed the healer's note meaningless, and requested a Western doctor's note in place of the healer's note to confirm Mmoledi's illness (South Africa: Supreme Court of Appeal, 2013). Mmoledi heeded her calling, and she left after her shift on June 1, 2007, to complete her *sangoma* training. In response, Kievits Kroon fired her.

Mmoledi brought the case before the South African Commission for Conciliation Mediation and Arbitration (CCMA), whose role is to handle labor-related disputes before they are escalated to the labor courts. The Commission ruled in Mmoledi's favor, finding that the decision was beyond her control, and her life was in danger if she didn't heed the call of her ancestors (Carrim, 2015). The Commission also cited that the summary rejection of the healer's note was the crux of the issue (South Africa: Supreme Court of Appeal, 2013). Had Kievits Kroon's staff treated the document as equivalent to a doctor's note or asked Mmoledi about the importance of the document, accommodations could have been made, including finding an alternate schedule arrangement. However, since that conversation never took place, and the healer's note was outright dismissed, Kievits Kroon was found in the wrong, and they were directed to reinstate Mmoledi.

The story doesn't end there. From 2008 to 2013, Kievits Kroon refused to comply with three court orders from the CCMA, the Labour Court of South Africa, and the Labour Appeal Court of South Africa, all of whom came to the same conclusion: Mmoledi should be reinstated. In

2013, the Supreme Court of Appeal concurred, ordering Kievits Kroon to reinstate Mmoledi and issuing a final word on the matter after five years of legal cases and opinion.

Mmoledi's story is an interesting example of workplace religious discrimination and eventual freedom due to the determination of the various courts. The rulings didn't state that Mmoledi should have immediately had her request accommodated as she stated it, but rather that the employer engaged in wrongful termination when they wholesale dismissed her request *because* it came from a *sangoma* and not a Western medical doctor. Had Kievits Kroon sought alternative accommodations or even discussed the note with Mmoledi, the courts maintained, there could have been an entirely different outcome (South Africa: Supreme Court of Appeal, 2013).

The courts' rulings reveal how South Africa grapples with religion and the workplace in the modern era. South Africa has been deeply engaged in a process of truth and reconciliation designed to help guide the nation forward from apartheid and the conflicts and human rights abuses that took place during that time. In the post-apartheid era, the practice of African indigenous religions has increased in South Africa. These religions were suppressed during apartheid, so an important part of national healing has included repositioning African indigenous religions and other non-Christian religions in conversations around employment. (Many Christian denominations, particularly the Dutch Reformed Church, played a large role in upholding apartheid and were allowed to practice their religion freely during apartheid, though there were also Christian organizations like the South African Council of Churches and people like Archbishop Desmond Tutu who organized against apartheid.) The Commission's and other courts' rulings in the Mmoledi case support the notion that religion isn't just something you do at home. To South Africans, dominant religions aren't the only ones that matter and impact the workplace.

Despite popular opinion to the contrary, religion is still alive and well—and growing across the world. Though there is some decline in religiosity in some countries in the global north—nearly 29% of adults in the U.S. don't identify with any religion according to the Pew Research Center (2021)—that doesn't negate that for many people in those countries and throughout the global south, religion is not just an important aspect of their lives, it's *the* most important aspect of their lives. We can observe this readily in the example of Mmoledi, who felt strongly that she must respond to her ancestors' call, even though she risked losing employment to do so. If there were no other examples—though there will be many throughout this book—Mmoledi alone proves that we do not live in an entirely post-religion era.

Even though we live in a time where many people are religious, our societies don't look like they used to in regard to religion. Due to many factors that we'll discuss in this chapter, religious diversity has become an important aspect of society and work.

When people think of diversity and inclusion in the workplace, the first identities that come to mind are typically gender and race. Of course, both are incredibly important aspects of who people are as individuals and how they show up at work. But for many religious people, religion is as important, if not more so, than any other aspect of their identity—and religious identity intersects with gender and race for many people. To both create a better world for all workers and to help our organizations perform better, we must understand all the aspects of identity that people bring to the workplace.

Understanding Religion and Religious Diversity

Religion is one of the concepts that everyone seems to understand implicitly, in part due to the history of how religions have formed and spread; yet there isn't one widely shared definition of religion. It's an elusive concept because religion is colloquially used to describe various cultural and social practices, beliefs, symbols, myths, and frameworks for meaning-making. Additionally, many conflate the term religion with one religion, for example, Christianity in the U.S., or a type of religious doctrine. Clarity on the meaning of the term may seem inconsequential, but as we discuss topics around religious diversity, it will be helpful to have a shared understanding. Carrim (2015) summarizes some definitions from the literature to describe religion as consisting of various devotional practices performed according to the teachings of a particular faith.

Although religion and spirituality are sometimes considered synonymous, they are distinct, and the differences between the two are illuminating. While religion entails adhering to a structured belief system, spirituality is concerned with growing into and experiencing the divine (Syed et al., 2017). The core distinction between spirituality and religion is that religion places emphasis on practices that are part of a belief system

(Byrd & Scott, 2014). While these differences exist, they are subtle and don't necessarily translate to a difference in experiences in the workplace. Another complex feature of religion is how it is often intertwined with ethnicity and sometimes racial identity. For many people whose ethnic and racial identities are connected to their religious identity, there isn't a distinction between the two, but rather an understanding of self that is inclusive of both. In many of these cases, religious identity isn't something communicated in physical appearance. The fact that many religious people do not wear distinctive religious garb or have physical appearances tied to their religion may account for the way religious diversity is neglected while gender, racial, and ethnic diversity is focused on in the workplace and society at large.

There are notable exceptions to this reality, though. In Chapter 4, we'll discuss, for instance, the experiences of Muslim women who wear the hijab at work and how they are treated. A Muslim woman might experience difficulties at the workplace because she's a woman, particularly if she wears the hijab, and if she's also a racial minority in the workplace. How do we quantify how much of that treatment is due to her religious identity versus her gender identity versus her racial identity? In fact, one Muslim woman said of her job seeking experiences, "It's hard to interpret interviews where I wasn't offered a job as being anti-woman vs. anti-hijab." (To learn more about other examples like this and my survey of Muslim women who wear the hijab, see Chapter 5.)

To recognize the validity and importance of these overlapping and intersecting identities, we must cultivate an intersectional lens. Intersectionality is a term coined by Kimberle Crenshaw (1989) to describe how Black women exist across categories that have in practice been treated as if they are mutually exclusive. Thus, in her example, the racism Black men experience and the sexism that white women experience *both differ* from the experiences of Black women whose lived realities are shaped by being both Black and women without a clear line between the two identities. By extension, for our purposes, intersectionality suggests that we must recognize the central nature of religion in the lives of religious people, many of whom are marginalized along other axes of identity that may shape their experiences. Furthermore, we cannot draw a line between the various identities an individual possesses, but rather, we must consider the person as a complex being.

Simply put, when religion is left out of the conversation, we neglect the whole. While religion has been neglected in many conversations about advancing diversity in organizations and communities, research shows that religious diversity in particular has been increasing (Alesina et al., 2003; Pew Research Center, 2014). In countries like the U.S., for example, the religious landscape is being transformed with the growth of religious traditions such as Islam, Hinduism, Buddhism, and Sikhism. Needless to say, this has implications for managing diversity at work.

While religious diversity is generally used to describe how different religions come together, there are sometimes elements of diversity within the same religion. Within the Christian religion, for example, there are about 6,000 denominations, many of which differ in basic tenets of their belief system (Carrim, 2015). Interestingly, intra-religion diversity at times can also lead to issues and challenges in the workplace. That said, individuals within the same broad religious group tend to understand one another and, despite differences, share more beliefs and practices than individuals outside that religion. As a result, workplace religious diversity focuses on differences between religions rather than differences between groups within the same religion.

Companies and individuals are increasingly interacting with individuals from diverse cultures, ethnicities, and religions (Syed et al., 2017). Thus, we are living in a more diverse society and working in more diverse workplaces. This marks a significant shift from the past when workplaces were much more homogenous across identities. However, not much attention has been placed on the role of religious diversity in the workplace and how this diversity should be managed to ensure inclusion.

Diverse workplaces stem from more diverse societies; this diversity is driven by globalization and increased global migration. Where globalization describes how companies, governments, and individuals interact, operate, and establish influence internationally, global migration describes how individuals move from one country to another, typically in search of work, though there are many reasons for migrating from one country to another (Czaika & De Haas, 2014).

While migration across international boundaries is not a new trend, the volume, diversity, and geographical scope of global migration has changed over the years due largely to increased globalization (Czaika & De Haas, 2014). By volume, for example, the number of global immigrants more than doubled over 50 years, from 92 million in 1960 to 222 million in 2010 (Ozden et al., 2011).

One new facet of global migration is how it has been enabled partly because of technological innovations in communication and transportation. It's easier than ever before to communicate across the globe, gain access to information about other countries, and move across borders in a number of ways. A cumulative effect of the ease of communication and movement has been an accelerated rate of global migration.

Global migration patterns have also become more complex (Czaika & De Haas, 2014). In the past, immigrants, especially economic immigrants, moved to countries with historical and colonial links. Immigrants from Anglophone African countries, for example, tended to migrate to England, while those from Francophone African countries preferred to move to France (Bakewell & De Haas, 2007). The same migration patterns could be seen between former colonizing countries and their so-called colonies. In recent decades, though, migrants from diverse origins have started selecting new destinations (Migration Policy Institute, 2020). More and more countries in Asia, for example, have become destinations for global immigrants due to their economic prosperity. The composition of immigrant populations has also shifted. Where the majority of immigrants used to be men in search of work accompanied by their families and dependents, today women, students, and asylum seekers are making up a larger portion of immigrant populations (Castles & Miller, 2009; Czaika & De Haas, 2014).

Immigration generally increases the diversity of a given society; this is not news (Collier, 2013; Putnam, 2007). Accelerated global migration, and to lesser degree rural–urban migration, has led to even more diverse societies and, by extension, workplaces. The complexity of modern global migration patterns further accentuates this diversity.

Historically, global migration moved in waves of homogenous groups immigrating to new locations, as in the case of the mass emigration from Europe to the Americas and other then-colonies. This form of migration typically led to less diverse societies. In regard to religion, that migration meant that the U.S. population, particularly white settlers who colonized and dominated the society they formed, has been to this point by and large Christian. As migration patterns change, the U.S. population is likewise changing, becoming more diverse in terms of religion. In the U.S. and beyond, modern global migration forms national populations that are diverse in terms of language, race, ethnicity, nationality of origin, and religion.

Despite this increased diversity across many axes, ethnic, and racial diversity dominate the conversation regarding the impact of immigration on societies and workplaces. While these important aspects of identity must be understood and embraced in the workplace, religious diversity also has significant impacts on employment, employee relations, and general management in the workplace. In a rather ironic manner, the dramatic increase in workplace discrimination reported by Muslims since the 9/11 attacks, as we'll discuss in-depth in Chapter 4, has brought more attention to the issue of workplace religious diversity and inclusion.

We must pay attention to the role religion plays in people's lives as we prepare for a more diverse workforce. Understanding religion, religions, and religious diversity lays the foundation for grappling with workplace religious diversity and the challenges it presents including discrimination. Before we can explore workplace religious discrimination in its own right, an understanding of the political and legal frameworks and protections for religious people is important.

THE RIGHT TO FREEDOM
OF RELIGION IN THE PUBLIC SPHERE

Freedom of religion is a right that has been guaranteed and codified by nations throughout the world in legal documents. These definitions are imperative for understanding the rights of religious people in the workplace; though none explicitly address the workplace, they do discuss religion in the public sphere, which is inclusive of the workplace in most cases.

At the international level, world agencies and institutions have produced rules and guides for the consideration of religion. For example, the United Nations (UN) Universal Declaration of Human Rights states in article 18:

> Everyone has the right to freedom of thought, conscience and religion; this right includes freedom to change his religion or belief, and freedom, either alone or in community with others and in public or private, to manifest his religion or belief in teaching, practice, worship and observance.

The Universal Declaration of Human Rights, proclaimed in Paris on December 10, 1948, was designed to establish a common standard of human rights for all nations and people. It is significant that religion is a protected class in this document, though the terms used in the clause above leave room for broad interpretation. The European Convention on Human Rights and the European Union (EU) Charter of Fundamental Rights, both designed to establish and protect basic human rights in constituent countries, have articles that protect the freedom of religion. Both align freedom of religion with freedom of thought and conscience.

In January 2016, over 250 Muslim religious leaders, scholars, and heads of state came together with members of various persecuted religious communities at a conference hosted by the king of Morocco to make the Marrakesh Declaration. The statement recognizes the rights of members of minority religions in predominantly Muslim countries and advocates the protection of these rights.

In addition to these international declarations, most countries have codified protections for religious rights in their constitutions and laws. For example, the basic rights of individuals to observe and express religious beliefs are firmly embedded within the U.S. Constitution and several federal statutes. The U.S. Constitution itself as well as two amendments to the constitution protect the rights of religious freedom explicitly. The First Amendment protects an individual's freedom of establishing and practicing a religion and prevents Congress from implementing a law that establishes a specific religion (Constitution Annotated, n.d.a). The 14th Amendment prevents any state from denying equal protection of the laws for all citizens of the United States (Constitution Annotated, n.d.b).

Two statutes also offer protection for freedom of religion in the U.S.: Title VII of the Civil Rights Act of 1964 and the Religious Freedom and Restoration Act of 1993 (RFRA). Title VII prohibits employers from discriminating against individuals on the basis of religion, color, race, sex, and national origin in all aspects of employment, including hiring, firing, and promotions. Title VII also requires employers to provide reasonable accommodation to an employee's religious needs, so long as the accommodation does not result in undue hardship to the employer. This statute covers all federal agencies and their employees, as are private businesses and state and local agencies that have fifteen or more employees (those employed for a certain period already). The RFRA statute, on the other hand, prevents the government from complicating an individual's right to exercise religion.

In part due to the language of these laws protecting religious freedom, religious freedom and inclusion is perceived to be more widespread than it is in practice. For instance, Workplace Fairness, a nonprofit that prides itself on providing comprehensive, unbiased information about the rights of workers, states on its website:

> The law protects not only people who belong to traditional organized religions such as Christianity, Islam, Judaism, or other faiths; but all people who have sincerely held religious, ethical, or moral beliefs.

This reflects a sentiment many people in the U.S. hold firmly; that religious freedom and inclusion are central to the U.S. society.

In contrast, when adults in the U.S. are polled by the Pew Research Center, they report seeing religious discrimination (Masci, 2019). In fact, 86% of respondents say Muslims are subject to at least some discrimination with a majority (56%) saying Muslims are discriminated against a lot. Sixty-four percent of respondents also say that Jewish people face at least some discrimination today, and half say the same is true for evangelical Christians. At the very least, this study reveals the contradicting perspectives of adults in the U.S. when it comes to religious discrimination, providing insight into the realities and perceptions of religious freedom.

Given the way these governing documents directly address the right to freedom of religion both nationally and internationally, it might seem like it would be simple to identify and prevent workplace religious discrimination. These laws and guidelines, however, rely on the principle of neutrality, which encourages religious freedom, but emphasizes not expressing religious beliefs and practices in the workplace (Hennette-Vauchez, 2017). Neutrality appears to only be aimed at curbing direct religious discrimination, and it is particularly prevalent in Europe where many cases of workplace religious discrimination have been referred to the European Court of Justice.

At first glance, the principle of neutrality in regard to religion in the workplace may look like a good solution to religious discrimination. In theory, neutrality could seem like it would lead to equal treatment. In reality, the principle of neutrality leads to exclusion, and doesn't discourage religious discrimination. In fact, it actually may even encourage that discrimination. The principle of neutrality also seems to be creating more uncertainty in the interpretation of extant laws in many European countries, rather than making the laws clearer. Paired with statutory language that is ambiguous, neutrality lends itself toward confusing and inconsistent interpretations of the law.

These varying interpretations of the legal frameworks in different countries are one of the greatest challenges facing workplace religious discrimination. In some cases, civic leaders, politicians, legislators, business owners, and individuals themselves are responsible for these interpretations:

- Giving lip service to religious freedom without engaging in meaningful work.
- Taking a hypocritical stance where *their* right to freedom of religion is protected, but others' is not because they're from a contradictory or marginalized religion.
- Lacking the political will to enforce the stated laws and frameworks, even when it's unpopular.

In some countries in Asia, for example, in spite of written commitments to existing international and regional laws and conventions on human rights, religious discrimination is still widespread, particularly in the case of minority religions (Williams, 2019). Fox (2020) argues that governments are responsible for enabling some religious discrimination, referring to this phenomenon as government-based religious discrimination. Whether or not the root of workplace religious discrimination is government-based, societal attributes and attitudes have a way of trickling down into the workplace.

Many existing legal frameworks do not specifically state what constitutes religious discrimination. That said, the U.S. Equal Employment Opportunity Commission (EEOC) clarifies what it considers to be religious discrimination: Under Title VII, employers are prohibited from showing bias for or against employees or potential employees due to their religious or spiritual identity, including those who have no religious or spiritual identity. This prohibition covers the continuum of hiring, promotion, compensation, employee classification, and dismissal of employees, even though the EEOC's definition does not constitute a legal, binding requirement. In January 2021, the EEOC issued revised guidance on workplace religious protections for the first time in thirteen years (Nagele-Piazza, 2021). Additional guidance and clarity were provided on religious-organization exemptions, reasonable accommodations and methods for accommodation, and special considerations for employers who must balance reasonable accommodations with antiharassment requirements (Nagele-Piazza, 2021).

Further complicating the matter is that legal regulations differ from country to country and, thus, so does the interpretation of what constitutes religious discrimination. Even within integrated regions, the determination of acts of religious discrimination are unclear and, in the case of the European Union, quite contentious. The task of defining workplace religious discrimination is made even more difficult by the fact that the same legal frameworks that protect against religious discrimination simultaneously protect some other rights such as the rights of businesses, clients, and customers, for example. Sometimes, protecting the religious rights of some persons may entail encroaching upon the rights of other persons or businesses. The question then is how to interpret the laws without infringement on anyone's rights. Assessing competing rights and interest is fundamental to defining acts of religious discrimination.

Another part of the challenge in defining workplace religious discrimination is the lack of clarity about and a wide variation between what is regarded to be religious discrimination generally and workplace religious discrimination specifically. Some variation in legal and political interpretation is typical, though the case of workplace religious discrimination is peculiar. Having looked at numerous cases and rulings, there appear to be no universal principles or application of existing international laws. When such principles exist in certain regions of the world, even their application ends up being largely subjective.

On July 15, 2021, for example, the Court of Justice of the European Union (CJEU), the highest European court, ruled on two cases brought before it by women from Germany. The CJEU ruled that employers can limit the expression of religious, political, and philosophical beliefs where there is "a genuine need" to "present a neutral image towards customers or to prevent social disputes" (Margolis, 2021).

This ruling mirrors the rulings on similar cases of religious freedom and discrimination in 2017 that was brought before the court from France and Belgium. In the case brought before the CJEU from France, a Muslim woman was fired from her job with an IT firm for wearing her hijab after a client's complaint (Hennette-Vauchez, 2017). In the case referred from Belgium to the CJEU, the company in question had informal internal rules that required workers to be neutral in religious, political, and philosophical matters. So, in many workplaces in Europe, there are no explicit HR policies to serve as guides on how to manage religious diversity and prevent religious discrimination (Equinet, 2018; Hennette-Vauchez, 2017). Typically, employers refer issues to the courts when incidents occur. The challenge that remains is that different courts continue to give different or contradictory rulings, even on cases with similar circumstances (Equinet, 2018). The inconsistency of how workplace religious discrimination is treated legally and politically increases the difficulty of enacting consistent, fair HR policies in the workplace.

To that end, defining workplace religious discrimination is paramount to understanding religious inclusion in the workplace.

UNDERSTANDING WORKPLACE RELIGIOUS DISCRIMINATION

Workplace religious discrimination is a phenomenon that arises because we have more diverse societies, and thus more diverse workplaces than ever before and at a time when religious intolerance is on the rise. Typically, religious discrimination increases when there is an identifiable majority in a homogenous religious group, and others outside the group, usually minorities, are perceived to be foreign to the homogenous majority (Fox, 2017).

The evidence of religious diversity globally has been firmly established (Alesina et al., 2003; Pew Research Center, 2014). Only about 16% of the world's population does not belong to a religion; the other 84% identify with one religious group or another. Furthermore, the number and percentage of the world population that is religious is projected to increase by 2050. Therefore, workplace religious diversity is not an ephemeral phenomenon, but rather a feature of the workplace that has come to stay. Despite this fact, the role and impact of religious discrimination in the workplace has not received much attention (Syed et al., 2017). (Little has changed since Syed and colleagues, and other researchers, made this assertion.)

Research on workplace religious diversity and inclusion, generally, is still only gaining momentum. As we've discussed, legal frameworks exist in many countries and the United Nations has conventions that, overall, aim to protect religious freedom, and prevent religious discrimination; however, it is still quite difficult to prevent workplace discrimination. Moreover, behaviors that constitute workplace religious discrimination are still largely not clear, and many organizations are grappling with understanding the issue of religious diversity and its management.

Notably, religious diversity in the workplace can lead to various challenges and problems, including:

- Conflicts between HR policies and employees' religious practices, a common occurrence (Mathis et al., 2016; Syed et al., 2017).
- Employees experiencing conflict with one another due to their religious differences (Byrd & Scott, 2014).
- Employees being required to conform to organization policies that conflict with their religion and beliefs (Gebert et al., 2014),
- Employees of diverse religious identities not wearing religious dress due to fear of not being hired, being rejected by colleagues, or other consequences (Reeves et al., 2012).
- Resentment between colleagues resulting from a lack of understanding of the beliefs and practices of different religions (Syed et al., 2017).

Effective management of religious diversity and prevention of discrimination to ensure inclusion is therefore vital in the workplace.

Unfortunately, religious discrimination in the workplace is rarely explicitly addressed in organization policies except when issues arise. Although it is becoming commonplace for organizations to proactively address religious discrimination in Western countries (Kirton & Greene, 2015), many organizations still do not explicitly address workplace religious discrimination until something goes wrong.

Religious discrimination is one of those acts that is easy to identify but difficult to define. It can range from microaggressions like stereotyping and negative labeling to outright harassment and physical victimization. One client I worked with, a scientist we'll call Tene, was encouraged not to share his religious beliefs with other scientists because it was assumed that his Christian faith was incongruent with science and reason. To try to allay some of these fears Tene stopped wearing a cross, and when asked what he did over the weekend, he stopped mentioning going to church. No one directly told him he had to hide his religion, but the social pressures he experienced made it clear he was supposed to be a scientist, not a Christian—and that the two were incongruent and thus Tene must choose. For example, when Tene picked up his child from daycare, she immediately noticed the crucifix was missing from his neck and asked where the beautiful necklace her grandmother had given him was. Tene felt conflicted and embarrassed; should he be loyal to his religion (and by extension, family) or should he be loyal to his workplace? Tene adapted to this environment by engaging in covering and downplaying an integral part of his identity to become more palatable to those around him. Covering is woefully common in the workplace and, while it is not always discrimination, it can be an indicator of discriminatory or at the least exclusionary practices.

Here are some useful definitions for workplace religious discrimination:

- Bowen (2010) asserts that religious discrimination exists "when certain individuals or groups do not enjoy the same rights and privileges as do members of other religious groups (or nonreligious people) in the society."
- Fox (2017) defines religious discrimination in reference to the differential treatment of minority religions as "restrictions placed on the religious practices and institutions of minority religions that are not placed on the majority religion."

Simply put, according to the various laws and conventions listed above, religious discrimination is any differential treatment resulting from religious beliefs or practices. This rather simple definition, nevertheless, is not as straightforward as it seems.

Based on the principle of neutrality, for example, legal frameworks of the European Union differentiate between direct and indirect religious discrimination. Direct religious discrimination is when a person is treated less favorably than others because of that person's religion or belief; indirect religious discrimination is when an apparent neutral policy or practice puts persons of a particular religion or belief at a disadvantage (Equinet, 2018). The principle of neutrality therefore only tries to negate direct religious discrimination. One can still be indirectly discriminated against, and the adjudication of whether such acts can be defined as religious discrimination is left to the discretion of the courts. Ultimately, defining religious discrimination boils down to the interpretation of existing laws by national and regional courts.

Despite the constitutional and legal safeguards that protect religious practices, religious discrimination continues to be a major challenge in the U.S. workplace (Ghumman et al., 2013). The issue of workplace religious discrimination is not limited to the U.S.. There has also been an increase in the number of cases of religious discrimination in Europe and Asia. In Europe, for example, the European Union has had to revisit the existing legal frameworks to guide against increasing religious intolerance (Equinet, 2018; Fox, 2017). Even in regions such as Asia where the religious landscape has been diverse for a long time (Kuhle, 2020), migration and urbanization are changing the dynamics of religious diversity.

Returning to the South African example of chef Johanna Mmoledi at the beginning of this chapter, organizations must prepare to deal with religious accommodation requests and do a better job of handling inclusion and discrimination cases related to traditional, non-Western religious who often constitute the religious outgroups. As Carrim (2015) reports, the post-apartheid era has ushered people from minority religions such as African indigenous religions and Hinduism into the workplace, and presented complex religious inclusion challenges to employers. As our world and the religious landscape in many countries continue to experience change, forward-thinking organizations must embrace the challenge of building a workplace culture that not only accommodates religious diversity and practices but one that is committed to driving change and progress.

References

Alesina, A., Devleeschauwer, A., Easterly, W., Kurlat, S., & Wacziarg, R. (2003). Fractionalization. *Journal of Economic Growth, 8*(2), 155–194.

Bakewell, O., & De Haas, H. (2007). African migrations: continuities, discontinuities and recent transformations. In P. Chabal, U. Engel, & L. de Haan (Eds.), *African alternatives* (pp. 95–118). Brill.

Bowen, J. R. (2010). Secularism: Conceptual genealogy or political dilemma. *Comparative Studies in Society and History, 52*(3), 680–694.

Byrd, M., & Scott, C. (2014). *Diversity in the workplace: Current issues and emerging trends.* Routledge.

Carrim, N. M. H. (2015) Managing religious diversity in the South African workplace. In S. Gröschl & R. Bendl (Eds.), *Religious diversity in the workplace* (pp. 113–136). Gower.

Castles, S., & Miller, M. J. (2009). *The age of migration.* Macmillan.

Collier, P. (2013). *Exodus. How migration is changing our world.* Oxford University.

Constitution Annotated. (n.d.a). *First amendment: Freedom of religion, speech, press, assembly, and petition.* https://constitution.congress.gov/browse/amendment-1/

Constitution Annotated. (n.d.b). *Fourteenth amendment: Citizenship, equal protection, and other post-civil war provisions.* https://constitution.congress.gov/browse/amendment-14/

Czaika, M., & De Haas, H. (2014). The globalization of migration: Has the world become more migratory? *International Migration Review, 48*(2), 283–323.

EEOC (2021, January 15). *Section 12: Religious discrimination.* https://www.eeoc.gov/laws/guidance/section-12-religious-discrimination

Equinet. (2018). *Faith in equality: Religion and belief in Europe.* Equinet European Network of Equality Bodies. https://equineteurope.org/faith-in-equality-religion-and-belief-in-europe/

Fox, J. (2017). Religious discrimination in European and Western Christian-majority democracies. *Journal for Religion, Society, and Politics, 1,* 185–209. https://doi.org/10.1007/s41682-017-0009-3

Fox, J. (2020). *Thou shalt have no other Gods before me: Why governments discriminate against minorities.* Cambridge University Press.

Gebert, D., Boerner, S., Kearney, E., King, J. E., Jr., Zhang, K., & Song, L. J. (2014). Expressing religious identities in the workplace: Analyzing a neglected diversity dimension. *Human Relations, 67*(5), 543–563.

Ghumman, S., Ryan, A. M., Barclay, L. A., & Markel, K. S. (2013). Religious discrimination in the workplace: A review and examination of current and future trends. *Journal of Business and Psychology, 28*(4), 439–454.

Hennette-Vauchez, S. (2017). Equality and the market: The unhappy fate of religious discrimination in Europe. *European Constitutional Law Review, Cambridge University Press, 13*(04), 744–758. https://doi.org/10.1017/S1574019617000359

Kirton, G., & Greene, A. (2015). *The dynamics of managing diversity: A critical approach.* Routledge.

Krenshaw, K. (1989). Demarginalizing the intersection of race and sex: A Black feminist critique of antidiscrimination doctrine, feminist theory and antiracist politics. *University of Chicago Legal Forum, 1989.* http://chicagounbound.uchicago.edu/uclf/vol1989/iss1/8

Kuhle, L. (2020). Conclusion. In J. Borup, M., Q. Fibiger, & L. Kuhle (Eds.), *Religious diversity in Asia* (pp. 317–331). Brill.

Marrakesh Declaration. (2016). *Declaration.* https://www.marrakeshdeclaration.org/index.html

Margolis, H. (2021, July 19). European Union court OKs bans on religious dress at work. *Human rights watch.* https://www.hrw.org/news/2021/07/19/european-union-court-oks-bans-religious-dress-work

Masci, D. (2019). Many Americans see religious discrimination in the US—especially against Muslims. *Pew Research Center*. https://www.pewresearch.org/fact-tank/2019/05/17/many-americans-see-religious-discrimination-in-u-s-especially-against-muslims/

Mathis, R., Jackson, J., & Valentine, S. (2016). *Human resource management: Essential perspective*. Cengage Learning.

Migration Policy Institute. (2020). *Top 25 destinations of international migrants*. https://www.migrationpolicy.org/programs/data-hub/charts/top-25-destinations-international-migrants

Nagele-Piazza, L. (2021). EEOC finalizes guidance on workplace religious protections. *SHRM*. https://www.shrm.org/resourcesandtools/legal-and-compliance/employment-law/pages/eeoc-finalizes-guidance-on-workplace-religious-protections.aspx

News24. (2013, December 5). *Triumph for traditional healers*. https://www.news24.com/health24/natural/natural-living/triumph-for-traditional-healers-20131205

Ozden, C., Parsons, C. R., Schiff, M., & Walmsley, T. L. (2011). Where on earth is everybody? The evolution of global bilateral migration 1960–2000. *The World Bank Economic Review, 25*(1), 12–56.

Pew Research Center. (2012). *The global religious landscape*. https://www.pewforum.org/2012/12/18/global-religious-landscape-exec/

Pew Research Center. (2014). *Global religious diversity*. https://www.pewforum.org/2014/04/04/global-religious-diversity/

Pew Research Center. (2021). *About three-in-ten U.S. adults are now religiously unaffiliated*. https://www.pewforum.org/2021/12/14/about-three-in-ten-u-s-adults-are-now-religiously-unaffiliated/

Putnam, R. D. (2007). E pluribus unum: Diversity and community in the twenty-first century, the 2006 Johan Skytte Prize lecture. *Scandinavian Political Studies, 30*(2), 137–174.

Reeves, T. C., McKinney, A. P., & Azam, L. (2012). Muslim women's workplace experiences: Implications for strategic diversity initiatives. *Equality, Diversity and Inclusion: An International Journal, 32*(1), 49–67. https://doi.org/10.1108/02610151311305614

South Africa: Supreme Court of Appeal. (2013). Kievits Kroon Country Estate (Pty) Ltd v Mmoledi and Others (South Africa Sup. Ct. of Appeal 2013). http://www.saflii.org/za/cases/ZASCA/2013/189

Syed, J., Klarsfeld, A., Ngunjiri, F. W., & Härtel, C.E.J. (2017). Introduction: The complex interface of work and religion. In *Religious diversity in the workplace*. Cambridge University Press.

United Nations. (1948). *Universal declaration of human rights*. https://www.un.org/en/about-us/universal-declaration-of-human-rights

Williams, N. (2019). The failure of the right to freedom of religion and belief?: The case of South East Asia. *Oxford Human Rights Hub*. https://ohrh.law.ox.ac.uk/the-failure-of-the-right-to-freedom-of-religion-and-belief-the-case-of-southeast-asia/

Workplace Fairness. (n.d.). *Religious discrimination*. https://www.workplacefairness.org/religious-discrimination

CHAPTER 3

The Benefits and Challenges of Embracing Religious Inclusion in the Workplace

Abstract While accommodating religious practices can pose complex challenges for organizations, there are immense benefits to embracing religious inclusion in an increasingly diverse world. In this chapter, the case is made for businesses to invest in diversity management, acknowledging the growth of a religiously affiliated population and embracing employees' religious beliefs and practices. This chapter describes initiatives to confront emerging global trends—secularism, radical right-party movements, and government restrictions on religious activity—that are threatening religious diversity in the workplace.

Keywords Business Case for Diversity · Immigration and diversity · Religious identity · Religious neutrality · Belonging

Restrictions on religious expression and religious symbols in public have become more common in Europe in recent years. According to Pew Research (2019a), in fact, while the highest levels of restrictions in the world exist in the Middle East and North Africa, the largest increases in certain types of restrictions actually took place in Europe. These increases appear in a few forms:

E. Hasan, *Embracing Workplace Religious Diversity and Inclusion*, Palgrave Studies in Equity, Diversity, Inclusion, and Indigenization in Business, https://doi.org/10.1007/978-3-030-89773-4_3

- Government restrictions on religious activity and dress
- Harassment of religious groups by the government
- Social hostility due to religious norms
- Organized groups using force or coercion to forward their own religious beliefs

Over the last decade or so, these restrictions have sharply increased (Pew Research, 2019a). They are often justified by calls to secularism and neutrality. In some cases, though, restrictions are accounted for by claims of protecting a country's way of life. For example, Geert Wilders, a Dutch parliamentarian, spoke publicly against Muslim populations in the West, bemoaning "a tsunami of refugees from Islamic countries who threaten our women and our civilization."

The restrictions on religious expression that are sweeping through Europe reveal the gap between our perception of protections of religious freedom and the lived reality for religious people. Many countries promise religious diversity and freedom in their laws and policies but in practice give preferential treatment to religious majorities or historically dominant religions and/or oppress religious minorities. Even when there aren't explicit restrictions on religion, one religion may be given preference over another due to factors including culture, the religious identity of political leaders or business elites. We'll explore this further in Part II.

In a world increasingly made up of diverse societies and organizations, diversity management has become a foremost issue. In the past, ethnic, gender, and racial diversity was the main focus of diversity management while religious diversity, and workplace religious diversity in particular, was neglected even after research established societies and workplaces were becoming more religiously diverse. Religious diversity sometimes carries a political undertone that is neither openly nor readily acknowledged, which may be a contributing factor in de-emphasizing religious diversity in the workplace. Moreover, some view religion as a matter of choice, a mutable characteristic, unlike other facets of one's identity like race and ethnicity. Finally, some contend that religion should be kept private and not be brought into the workplace.

These assertions do not grapple with the reality that the world has become more religious over time. It is true that there are more people (in number) that are unaffiliated with any religion than ever before. That figure moved from 0.71 billion in 1970 to 1.2 billion in 2015. At the same time, the 6.21 billion people affiliated with one religion or the other

Table 3.1 World's Major Religions

By Population (In Billions)				
	1970	2010	2015	2050 (Projection)
Christians	1.23	2.17	2.3	2.92
Muslims	0.57	1.60	1.8	2.76
Unaffiliated	0.71	1.13	1.2	1.23
Other Religions	0.49	0.46	0.51	0.53
Hindus	0.46	1.03	1.1	1.38
Buddhists	0.23	0.49	0.50	0.49
Total	**3.69**	**6.88**	**7.41**	**9.31**
Religiously Affiliated vs. Unaffiliated (In Billions)				
	1970	2010	2015	2050 (Projection)
Religiously Affiliated	2.98	5.75	6.21	8.08
Unaffiliated	0.71	1.13	1.2	1.23
Total	**3.69**	**6.88**	**7.41**	**9.31**
By Population (%)				
	1970	2010	2015	2050 (Projection)
Christians	33.33	31.54	31.04	31.36
Muslims	15.45	23.26	24.29	29.65
Unaffiliated	19.24	16.42	16.19	13.21
Other Religions	13.28	6.67	6.88	5.69
Hindus	12.47	14.97	14.84	14.82
Buddhists	6.23	7.12	6.75	5.26
Religiously Affiliated vs. Unaffiliated (%)				
	1970	2010	2015	2050 (Projection)
Religiously Affiliated	80.76	83.56	83.80	86.79
Unaffiliated	19.24	16.42	16.19	13.21

Source Based on data from Pew Research Center (2015) and Brian J. Grim (2015)

still made up nearly 84% of the world population in 2015 (Pew Research, 2017). According to some data on world religions (see Table 3.1), the population of religiously affiliated people is projected to increase to 8.08 billion or over 86% of world population by 2050 (Pew Research, 2017).

It is clear that the number of people affiliated with a religion is increasing much more rapidly than those without any religious affiliation. The percentage of the religiously unaffiliated worldwide has been decreasing since 1970, and it is projected to continue to decrease to about 13% in 2050.

The data shows that the issue of workplace religious diversity is not going away any time soon. More and more people will become affiliated with at least one religion in the future. In short, religious affiliation is increasing and workplaces are becoming more religiously diverse. Given this trend, continuing to exclude religious diversity and inclusion from workplace diversity management considerations would neglect an incredibly important identity for many people and a large identity group.

Additionally, though it can often be viewed as a source of tension, workplace religious diversity can also be a source of values conducive to workplace performance, as we'll discuss in the next section. Beyond the business, legal, and moral cases for embracing and including workplace religious identity in diversity and inclusion efforts that we've discussed, there is a practical argument for including religion at work as an untapped resource for better individual and group performance.

Religious Diversity, Inclusion, and Belonging at Work

At a time when diversity and inclusion efforts are encouraging workers to bring their whole selves into the workplace, it should be no surprise that religion is one of the aspects of self showing up at work. In recognition of this fact, there has been a rise in research on religion and spirituality in the workplace, focused on describing, measuring, and assessing both the challenges and significant opportunities religion and spirituality present in the workplace (Fry, 2013; Syed et al., 2017). We discussed the potential challenges of workplace religious diversity at length in Chapter 2. In contrast to those challenges, spirituality and religion bring numerous benefits to the workplace, including:

- Useful and relevant business and managerial practices drawn from religious practices and beliefs (Syed et al., 2017).
- Increased productivity among individuals who are religious (Ecklund et al., 2020).
- More optimism about upward mobility in the workplace (Reynolds et al., 2019).
- Increased work ethic, motivation, and commitment (Affeldt & MacDonald, 2010; Anwar & Osman-Gani, 2015).
- Enhanced leadership skills (Cowan, 2005).

- Engaging in activities beyond their job descriptions that contribute positively to the workplace, also known as organizational citizenship behaviors (Affeldt & MacDonald, 2010).
- Increased perception of one's work having meaning or purpose (Bellah et al., 1985; Dik & Duffy, 2009).

Of course, these factors together contribute to organizational performance and further support the business case for diversity management including religious diversity.

In practice, more organizations, including both those that are faith-based and those that are fully secular, are recognizing the important role of religion in the workplace. Religious inclusion is on the organizational agenda, with organizations finding ways to accommodate their religious employees of various faiths and enacting policies and practices that are more inclusive of religions that may not be mainstream (SHRM, 2008). Though accommodations are prevalent in Western countries, multinational companies are adopting these practices at the global level and finding that such accommodations reduce tension and conflict for religious workers.

These factors make it clear how important religious inclusion in the workplace truly is. We've already been using the term inclusion in this book, and it may be familiar as it has gained prominence in recent years, but it's important to break down the concept. In fact, I believe inclusion is so important that rather than talking about diversity, equity, and inclusion (collectively called DEI), I believe in focusing on inclusion, diversity, and equity, which I call IDE. It may seem like a minor issue, but the truth is that when we lead with the concept of diversity, that's often where the work stops. But if we focus first on inclusion—on making our workplaces better, safer, and more engaging places for people of all religious backgrounds and none—then we are ready for the reality of diversity as it arrives.

My point here is that whereas diversity is a fact of life—and naturally occurring—inclusion is a choice, and requires deliberate action. As IDE expert Verna Myers aptly put it, "Diversity is being invited to the party. Inclusion is being asked to dance." I would go one step further. If you've been invited to the party and asked to dance, asking you to choose the song and making you feel free to dance how you want to is empowering. It is about *feeling* like you are part of a community where your various identities are welcomed, respected, and appreciated. That's the power of belonging.

When Farah Alhajeh was a candidate for a job with a translation company called Semantix based in Sweden, she was offered a handshake by a male interviewer (McCulloch, 2018). Alhajeh smiled, declined to shake hands, and offered a greeting by placing her hand on her heart. She explained that her religion required her to avoid physical contact with the interviewer. Her interviewer responded by cutting off the interview and abruptly directing her to leave. Alhajeh was left in tears, feeling completely disrespected and caught off guard. Two years later, a Swedish labor court ruled in Alhajeh's favor, finding that her refusal to shake hands was a religious manifestation protected by the European Convention on Human Rights. Alhajeh was awarded $4,500 in compensation.

In regard to our wider conversation on workplace religious diversity, Alhajeh's story shows that the fact of diversity—she is a Swedish Muslim woman—was not met by an act of inclusion, which in this case would look like accepting the greeting offered by Alhajeh in lieu of a handshake. In a workplace where belonging is the focus, the interviewer could accept the greeting at the moment, even if he didn't understand it, and then take time to learn more about Muslim practices to ensure he could create an environment of belonging for current and future Muslim employees. Alhajeh's terrible experience at her job interview, years of legal proceedings, and thousands in compensation all could have been avoided had belonging driven the culture at Semantix.

There are numerous ways to accommodate religious practices in the workplace beyond Alhajeh's example, including:

- Providing flexible work schedules. Many religions require regular prayer or observance of a holy day. For instance, Seventh Day Adventist Christians observe the sabbath on Saturdays and thus would need to be excluded from Saturday work shifts.
- Creating designated places for religious activities. In some cases, it isn't practical to wait to get home for prayer, so having a space designated for individual or group prayer is important. For example, some Muslims pray five times a day, including while at work, and thus need a designated space for their religious observance. Many companies call these spaces quiet rooms (Career Trend, 2018).
- Recognizing diverse religious holidays. As we've discussed, many nations recognize the Christian holiday of Christmas but do not

recognize any other religion-affiliated holidays. An employer with a focus on belonging will allow employees to take off for their holidays, even when it doesn't coincide with other state or national holidays.

- Allowing religious expression in the workplace. While bans on religious expression have increased, employers can choose to allow employees to express their religion freely in dress and displays of religious symbols on themselves and in their private work spaces.
- Allowing religious expression between employees. Many workplaces discourage the discussion of religion at work, in part due to a fear of colleagues trying to convert one another. However, if you make clear that the workplace isn't a place for proselytization, but rather for exchange, you can provide a place for employees to get to know one another at a deeply meaningful level. (Check out Chapter 6 for further exploration of this concept.)

Embracing the whole person at work, inclusive of their religious identity, may seem like a challenge, but it's one that yields results.

A significant number of your employees, your colleagues, and your constituents are religious people. When we fail to cultivate a sense of belonging for those individuals, we lose out on the best they have to offer our workplaces and our societies.

Emerging Global Trends Shaping Workplace Religious Diversity

Global trends around religion and spirituality have an impact on the workplace and how workers with diverse religious beliefs and affiliations are treated. There are a number of emerging trends that impact this conversation in various ways.

Secularism and Religious Pluralism

At one time, the major religion in most Western nations in Europe and North America, as well as Australia, was Christianity. Historically, these nations integrated religion into the state, and had civic officials who were representatives of the church and vice versa. There truly was no separation of the two spheres. Today, most of these countries are secular states where religious institutions are officially separated from the state. Secularism has become more commonplace, and in some cases has laid a foundation for religious pluralism.

In simple terms, religious pluralism is the recognition that there is virtue in all religions and that they have equal value. Religious pluralism is not merely the awareness of diverse religions but also the acknowledgment of the different beliefs and belief systems that exist (Basinger, 2020). It is also the recognition of both theistic and atheistic beliefs, and the wide variety within and between these two main kinds of belief systems. Religious pluralism connotes religious freedom; the free will to choose and practice any theistic and atheistic belief system. In principle, secularism and religious pluralism are embedded into the legal frameworks of Western countries, which are purportedly endearing to religious freedom.

There is a subtle assumption that increased religious pluralism leads to religious acceptance. Unfortunately, this is not always the case in reality. While religious pluralism may be an acceptance of religious diversity, it does not necessarily automatically lead to religious inclusion. For example, some parochial schools supported by Christian churches have a practice of hiring people of diverse religious backgrounds. Sadly, that hiring practice often doesn't translate to inclusion and belonging. So, though a new hire may be accepted, they are still viewed as other and as not belonging to the team due to their religious beliefs and practices.

Indeed, the growing awareness of diverse religions in many Western countries has not led to increased religious inclusion. Secularism may have created space for religious pluralism and religious freedom, but it has not necessarily promoted religious inclusion. The freedom to express one's religious beliefs in some practices such as wearing a crucifix, for example, has caused tension in workplaces in some Western countries. This shows that achieving religious inclusion in the workplace requires a deliberate and strategic effort. It is neither an accidental nor a direct and immediate consequence of growing secularism and religious pluralism, nor even religious freedom.

In some parts of the world where governments favor specific religions, secularism and religious pluralism are still unfamiliar ideas. Consequently, in these places, such as countries in the Middle East, religion and the state are still intertwined, and the concept of religious freedom is still far-fetched. These world regions have been less affected by the immigration of people with diverse religious beliefs. In many cases, workplace religious discrimination, and religious discrimination in the wider society, are not given much focus even when religious diversity exists due to the politics of the state religion.

Religious Rights and Equality Movements

All over the world, there has been a proliferation of organizations and movements defending, promoting, and protecting human rights. Most of these focus on gender and racial equality, including feminism and the Black Lives Matter movement. These movements help bring other issues of diversity into the conversation as people organize more differently than ever before.

Religious rights movements present a particular challenge. Religion-based movements can sometimes serve as political instruments bringing about both positive and negative outcomes for individuals and society as a whole. This sort of double-edged movement can be observed throughout history, as human rights and religion have often been at odds. People have killed and discriminated against others—human rights violations—because of the incompatibility of their religious beliefs (Fortman, 2011).

There is also some question of friction between individual religious beliefs and protecting the rights of all religious people. For example, if a religion states that it is the only true religion, is an adherent betraying their religion by supporting people of other religions to express their beliefs? The response to this question isn't universal and, because of this, many religious rights organizations tread carefully to ensure that the fundamental human rights of others are protected even as they fight to protect their own religious freedom and rights.

Integral to the religious equality movements are Non-Government Organizations (NGOs), which can provide useful platforms for religious civil rights and advocacy. Unsurprisingly, these organizations are mostly found in Western and developed countries with high levels of religious diversity, and where most of the diverse religions are as a result of immigration. These NGOs work to bring attention to the need for more religious tolerance, seeking to protect victims of religious discrimination. They denounce such violations, and generally monitor the situation of religious discrimination and intolerance in their jurisdictions.

NGOs face various challenges from needing to differentiate themselves from faith- and religion-based organizations that seek their own religion-specific goals to facing additional governmental scrutiny due to their perceived similarities with clandestine operations using the guise of NGOs as a cover (Hodwitz, 2016; Ly, 2007). They also must keep the politics of their organizations separate from their religious rights and advocacy work.

Regardless, the growth of these human rights organizations fighting for religious rights and freedom is bringing much-needed attention to workplace religious diversity and discrimination.

Radical Right-Party Movements

Just as there are encouraging global trends emerging, there are concerning ones as well. As movements to advance human rights and equality across axes of identity rise, so too do reactionary movements against human rights and equality. Reactionary movements such as Islamophobia and Islamist radicalism, white supremacy movements, and xenophobia have recently increased; all reject human rights and equality (Syed & Ozbilgin, 2020). Vassilopoulou and colleagues (2019) argue that these reactionary movements are in some ways an indirect aftermath of global political events such as the global financial crisis that undermined economic growth in many countries between 2007 and 2009 and the withdrawal of the UK from the European Union, commonly referred to as Brexit. Regardless, these reactionary movements have the tendency to fuel discrimination, promote nationalism, and increase xenophobia. These movements may be responsible for increases in religious discrimination throughout Europe.

Radical or far right political parties represent one reactionary movement that is gaining prominence in the political landscape and becoming increasingly accepted by the populace, at least in part due to their stance against immigration. Disturbingly, in Austria, Belgium, Denmark, Estonia, Finland, Hungary, Italy, Spain, Sweden, and Switzerland, Nationalist far right parties received about 15% more votes in European Parliament elections and opinion polls (BBC, 2019; Lavis & Deole, 2017).

Growing anti-immigration sentiments fuel the success of contemporary far right parties in Europe (e.g., see Becker & Fetzer, 2016; Dustmann et al., 2016; Edo & Giesing, 2020; Halla et al., 2017; Lavis & Deole, 2017; Otto & Steinhardt, 2014). Many of the people lured by these extremist parties complain that European countries are too diverse. They blame immigrants for the economic hardships that have continued in the years since the global recession and financial crisis of 2007, saying it is due to high levels of immigration (BBC, 2019; Edo & Giesing, 2020; Lavis & Deole, 2017).

Immigration has increased in Europe, in no small part due to shifting global migration patterns, as we discussed in Chapter 2. There is no doubt that between 2002 and 2014, the immigrant population in most European countries grew by over 50% (Lavis & Deole, 2017; OECD, 2016). Furthermore, European governments have struggled to put in place policies that effectively manage high immigration and the economy (Lavis & Deole, 2017). Undoubtedly, anti-immigration sentiments are not favorable to the promotion of religious diversity and inclusion either in the society or the workplace, or even to other forms of diversity.

Unfortunately, radical right-party movements are not going away, and though we've spoken exclusively about their rise in Europe in this section, these movements are rising throughout the global north *and* the global south.

Religious Tensions Around the World

As we discussed at the opening of this chapter, religious restrictions and tensions have increased in Europe. In reality, although the level of restrictions on religious beliefs and practices is higher in some places around the globe than in others, many countries have some level of religious restriction. The number of countries with the highest levels of religious restrictions rose from 40 in 2007 to 52 in 2017 (PEW Research, 2019b).

Religious restrictions are at the highest levels both in law and practice in the Middle East and North Africa (PEW Research, 2019b). Some countries in Asia also have some forms of religious restrictions in practice, though they are not usually explicitly stated in laws. Even in cases where explicit laws protect religious freedom, religious restrictions persist (Finke, 2013). In the case of the Middle East and North Africa, restrictions stem mainly from explicit state support for one religion. In contrast, in many Latin American countries, state support for one religion is more subdued, implicit, informal, and based on past traditions (Finke, 2013). You might guess that religious restrictions in the Middle East and North Africa are targeted at minority religions, but that isn't necessarily the case. Even within the major religion in this world region—Islam—there are restrictions placed upon certain sects (PEW Research, 2019c).

Restrictions range from government laws and policies restricting religious freedom and activities to favoring one religious group over others (PEW Research, 2019b, 2019c). Notably, restrictions on religious dress and symbols in public have become more common:

- Countries including Belgium, Bulgaria, and France, and some local regions in Germany, Italy, Russia, Spain, and Switzerland have banned the wearing of religious dress in one form or another, notably face veils (BBC, 2018).
- In 2011, France became one of the first countries to ban the wearing of full-face coverings in the public in Europe.
- Bill 21 is a law in place in the Quebec Province of Canada. Passed in June 2019, the law bans public servants from wearing crucifixes, yarmulkes, hijab, and other religious dresses and symbols in the workplace. Efforts by some religious rights and liberties movements to upend the law through higher courts in Canada have so far been unsuccessful. In April 2021, a top Quebec court upheld the provisions of Bill 21.
- Britain and the Netherlands have also considered banning religious attire like the hijab in public places.
- In the People's Republic of China, over 1 million Uyghurs, a predominantly Muslim ethnic group indigenous to Northwest China, have been incarcerated in "re-education camps" designed to make Uyghurs into "reformed" Chinese people without Muslim beliefs. Other Chinese Muslims have also been sent to these camps (Hammond, 2021).

Some of these laws and prohibitions come with fines and penalties for noncompliance; others have much higher stakes. Although most of these bans are said to be neutral, aimed at promoting a secular society and not targeted at any particular religion, the frequent impetus for the bans has been the debate on Muslim women wearing the hijab, especially in Europe. Of course, these tensions boil over into the workplace where Muslim women in hijabs have had their headscarves ripped off their heads by colleagues emboldened by public debate and perception.

You might be surprised to learn that the ban on religious dress and symbols has not been limited to non-Islamic majority countries. Tunisia, Turkey, and Syria have gone back and forth on the debate and ban on religious dress, each at one time or another banning the wearing of face veils for security concerns.

Security concerns come up again and again as part of the justification of these bans. At the same time, bans impede religious freedom and violate individuals' religious liberties. As you can see, the arguments for and against bans on religious dress and symbols raise questions about the interplay of different fundamental human rights. This interplay also takes place in workplace conversations regarding religious diversity, even in the case where the ban does not explicitly address the workplace. For instance, in the case of Samira Achbita and her dispute with her Belgium-based employer, G4S Secure Solutions, regarding her dismissal for wearing her hijab, the CJEU ruled that dress code rules relating to restriction of religious attire in the workplace do not constitute direct discrimination (Equinet, 2018). It doesn't feel like a stretch to say the private employer was likely influenced by existing bans on religious dress in Belgium.

Many cases of religious discrimination have been taken to courts both in countries where there are and are not bans on religious dress and symbols. As we discussed in Chapter 2, the challenge lies mostly in the interpretation of existing laws by the courts. Since 2017, when the first cases on religious discrimination were brought before it, the CJEU has delivered a dozen judgments on similar cases with many still pending (Witte & Pin, 2021). Religious discrimination cases are, however, not limited to corporate workplaces. Court cases related to workers in schools and hospitals have also increased, pointing to the spread of a more religiously diverse society.

These major global trends reveal how seemingly divergent events and trends are converging to bring the issue of workplace religious diversity to the fore. While some of the issues are positively influencing the management of religious diversity and aiding religious inclusion in the workplace, others seem to be having a negative influence.

The opportunities and threats inherent in these global trends, especially to the management of business organizations, are manifold:

- Increasing expression of religion and spirituality in the workplace brings with it the opportunities of creating alternative approaches to work and management, creating awareness of the need for strategic management of religious diversity in the workplace, and helping organizations be more responsive to an increasingly religiously diverse customer base. At the same time, if not managed well, this expression could lead to conflicts in the workplace, with employees going overboard with their religious expression.

- Secularism, religious pluralism, and religious freedom promote acceptance and equal treatment of all employees inclusive of religion, and it could promote religious tolerance rather than inclusion if the principle of neutrality is unexamined.
- Religious rights and equality movements help workers develop knowledge of their rights and protect those rights, but in some cases, this could lead to impeding the rights of others.
- Radical right-party movements reveal existing tensions that must be addressed by leaders at work and in society. These movements also promote religious and other forms of discrimination, which could lead to disunity in the workplace and keep organizations from utilizing an incredible resource: workers of foreign origin. These movements could also deter organizations from engaging in foreign investments, products, and services.
- Religious restrictions prevent ambiguity regarding accepted expressions of religious beliefs and practices in the workplace, and they can make creating HR policies in alignment with those restrictions simpler. That said, these restrictions almost inevitably lead to impeding on employees' religious rights, creating conflicts in the workplace and forcing employees to cover their religion rather than bringing their whole selves into the workplace.

These trends help create awareness of workplace religious diversity and the need for religious inclusion as the world and workplaces become more religious.

Many challenges and opportunities arise when it comes to religious diversity, inclusion, and belonging in the workplace. We've explored the roots of these challenges and opportunities, what they allow or prevent in society, and the wider implications of the global trends currently emerging. Now it's time to explore the reality of managing workplace religious diversity and inclusion in various contexts throughout the world.

References

Affeldt, D. L., & MacDonald, D. A. (2010). The relationship of spirituality to work and organizational attitudes and behaviors in a sample of employees from a healthcare system. *The Journal of Transpersonal Psychology, 42*(2), 192–208.

Anwar, M. A., & Osman-Gani, A. M. (2015). The effects of spiritual intelligence and its dimensions on organizational citizenship behavior. *Journal of Industrial Engineering and Management, 8*(4), 1162–1178.

Basinger, D. (2020). Religious diversity (pluralism). *The Stanford encyclopedia of philosophy* (Edward N. Zalta, Ed., Winter 2020 ed.). https://plato.stanford.edu/archives/win2020/entries/religious-pluralism/

BBC. (2019, November 13). *Europe and right-wing nationalism: A country by country guide.* https://www.bbc.com/news/world-europe-36130006

BBC. (2018, May 31). *The Islamic veil across Europe.* https://www.bbc.com/news/world-europe-13038095

Becker, S. O., & Fetzer, T. (2016). *Does migration cause extreme voting?* (Warwick Working Paper Series 306). https://econpapers.repec.org/paper/cgewacage/306.htm

Bellah, R. N., Madsen, R., Sullivan, W. M., Swidler, A., & Tipton, S. M. (1985). *Habits of the heart: Individualism and commitment in American life.* University of California Press.

Career Trend. (2018, December 31). *What is a quiet room at work?* https://careertrend.com/quiet-room-work-5171.html

Cowan, D. A. (2005). Translating spiritual intelligence into leadership competences. *Journal of Management, Spirituality & Religion, 2*(1), 3–38.

Dik, B. J., & Duffy, R. D. (2009). Calling and vocation at work: Definitions and prospects for research and practice. *The Counseling Psychologist, 37*(3), 424–450. https://doi.org/10.1177/0011000008316430

Dustmann, C., Vasiljeva, K., & Piil, A. (2016). *Refugee migration and electoral outcomes* (CReAM Discussion Paper Series CPD 19/16). https://econpapers.repec.org/paper/crmwpaper/1619.htm

Ecklund, E. H., Daniels, D., Bolger, D., & Johnson, L. (2020) A nationally representative survey of faith and work: Demographic subgroup differences around calling and conflict. *Religions, 11*(287). https://doi.org/10.3390/rel11060287

Edo, A., & Giesing, Y. (2020). *Has immigration contributed to the rise of right-wing extremist parties in Europe?* (Economic Policy Report No 23, European Network for Economic and Fiscal Policy Research). University of Munich, Munich. https://www.ifo.de/DocDL/EconPol_Policy_Report_23_Immigration_Far_Right.pdf

Equinet. (2018). *Faith in equality: Religion and belief in Europe.* Equinet European Network of Equality Bodies. https://equineteurope.org/faith-in-equality-religion-and-belief-in-europe/

Finke, R. (2013). Origins and consequences of religious restrictions: A global overview. *Sociology of Religion, 74*(3), 297–313. https://doi.org/10.1093/socrel/srt011

Fortman, B. G. (2011). *Religion and human rights: A dialectical relationship.* https://www.e-ir.info/2011/12/05/religion-and-human-rights-a-dialectical-relationship/

Fry, L. (2013). Spiritual leadership and faith and spirituality in the workplace. In J. Neal (Ed.), *Handbook of faith and spirituality in the workplace* (pp. 697–704). Springer.

Grim, B. J. (2015). How religious will the world be in 2050? *World Economic Forum.* https://www.weforum.org/agenda/2015/10/how-religious-will-the-world-be-in-2050/

Halla, M., Wagner, A. F., & Zweimüller, J. (2017). Immigration and voting for the far right. *Journal of the European Economic Association, 15*(6), 1341–1385. https://doi.org/10.2139/ssrn.2103623

Hammond, K. (2021). The terrible 'Sinicization' of Islam in China. *New Lines Magazine.* https://newlinesmag.com/argument/the-terrible-sinicization-of-islam-in-china/

Hodwitz, O. (2016). NGO interventions: influences on terrorist activity. *Behavioral Sciences of Terrorism and Political Aggression, 10,* 1–26.

Lavis, D., & Deole, S. S. (2017). Immigration and the rise of far-right parties in Europe. *Leibniz Institute for Economic Research, University of Munich, DICE Report, 15*(4), 10–15.

Ly, P. (2007). The charitable activities of terrorist organizations. *Public Choice, 131*(1/2), 177–195.

McCulloch, A. (2018, August 17). Swedish woman compensated after job interview handshake refusal. *Personnel Today.* https://www.personneltoday.com/hr/job-interview/

OECD. (2016). *International migration outlook.* Organisation for Economic Co-Operation and Development (OECD) Publishing.

Otto, A. H., & Steinhardt, M. F. (2014). Immigration and Election outcomes: Evidence from City Districts in Hamburg. *Regional Science and Urban Economics, 45*(1), 67–79.

Pew Research Center. (2015). *Muslims.* https://www.pewforum.org/2015/04/02/muslims/

Pew Research Center. (2017). *Christians remain the largest religious group but they are declining in Europe.* https://www.pewresearch.org/fact-tank/2017/04/05/christians-remain-worlds-largest-religious-group-but-they-are-declining-in-europe/

Pew Research Center. (2019a). *Europe experienced a surge in government restrictions on religious activity over the last decade.* https://www.pewresearch.org/fact-tank/2019a/07/29/europe-experienced-a-surge-in-government-restrictions-on-religious-activity-over-the-last-decade/

Pew Research Center. (2019b). *Middle East still home to highest levels of restrictions on religion, although levels still declined since 2016.* https://www.pewforum.org/2019b/07/15/middle-east-still-home-to-highest-levels-of-res trictions-on-religion-although-levels-have-declined-since-2016/

Pew Research Center. (2019c). *A closer look at how religious restrictions have arisen around the world.* https://www.pewforum.org/2019c/07/15/a-clo ser-look-at-how-religious-restrictions-have-risen-around-the-world/

Reynolds, J., May, M., & Xian, H. (2019). Not by bread alone: Mobility experiences, religion, and optimism about future mobility. *Socius: Sociological Research for a Dynamic World, 5,* 1–15. https://doi.org/10.1177/237802 3119849807

SHRM. (2008). *Religion and corporate culture: Accommodating religious diversity in the workplace.* https://www.shrm.org/hr-today/trends-and-forecasting/res earch-and-surveys/documents/08-0625religionsr_updtfinal.pdf

Syed, J., & Ozbilgin, M. (2020). Introduction: Understanding and managing diversity and inclusion in the global workplace. In J. Syed & M. F. Ozbilgin (Eds.), *Managing diversity and inclusion: An international perspective.* Sage.

Syed, J., Klarsfeld, A., Ngunjiri, F. W., & Härtel, C. E. J. (2017). Introduction: The complex interface of work and religion. In J. Syed, A. Klarsfeld, F. Wambura Ngunjiri, & C. E. J. Hartel (Eds), *Religious diversity in the workplace* (pp. 1–34). Cambridge University Press.

Vassilopoulou, J., Kyriakidou, O., Da Rocha, J. P., Georgiadou, A., & Barak, M. M. (2019). International perspectives on securing human and social rights and diversity gains at work in the aftermath of the global economic crisis and in times of austerity. *European Management Review, 16,* 837–845.

Witte, J. J., & Pin, A. (2021). Faith in Strasbourg and Luxembourg? The fresh rise of religious freedom litigation in the Pan-European Courts. *Emory Law Journal, 70*(3), 587.

PART II

ERGs, IDE Strategies, and Leadership: Managing Workplace Religious Diversity and Inclusion

CHAPTER 4

Evaluating Religious Inclusion and Belonging

Abstract It is unacceptable that religion remains a largely neglected component of workplace diversity, equity, inclusion, and belonging (DEIB) initiatives. True commitment to the pursuit of DEIB maturity requires a holistic approach that embraces religious identity as well as diversity accountability. Evidence of religious inclusion maturity can be measured in a four-level model: (1) Avoidance, (2) Compliance, (3) Emerging, and (4) Transformational. This chapter's case study of Chobani's experience with Muslim refugees serves as a prototype for advancing from levels 1 and 2 (where most organizations appear to be concentrated) to levels 3 and 4.

Keywords Kaizen HC model of religious inclusion · Refugee Inclusion · Diversity hiring · Diversity accountability · Workplace belonging

In late 2016, Hamdi Ulukaya, the founder and billionaire owner of Chobani, came under fire for his practice of hiring refugees. Beyond criticism, Ulukaya also began to receive death threats alongside outlandish accusations from far right news media that he was vowing to choke [the] U.S. with Muslims. Thankfully, it was not all negative publicity. At the same time that some rallied to boycott and send hate toward Chobani,

E. Hasan, *Embracing Workplace Religious Diversity and Inclusion*, Palgrave Studies in Equity, Diversity, Inclusion, and Indigenization in Business, https://doi.org/10.1007/978-3-030-89773-4_4

customers rallied to support Chobani on social media and by making the yogurt company's products a part of their regular grocery shopping (Pathak, 2016).

Part of the reason Ulukaya, Chobani, and Muslim refugees had come into the spotlight was the 2016 U.S. presidential election during which Republicans and the far right used Chobani and its Twin Falls, Idaho factory as evidence to stoke fear and resentment toward Muslims and refugees. In reality, the factory was and is partly staffed by refugees, some of whom are Muslim and some who are not—all of whom had been resettled by the U.S. government. Furthermore, Chobani's first, much smaller factory in upstate New York had already utilized similar hiring policies, turning to refugees who had been settled in Utica, New York, to help staff its factory. Ulukaya provided them with transportation and translators working on the factory floor to assist workers. So, when he decided to build a larger factory in Twin Falls, Ulukaya figured he had a chance of making an even bigger impact, creating 1,000 jobs and helping Twin Falls become a thriving town.

While outsiders turned the small town and Chobani's policy of hiring refugees into a political spectacle, Idaho Governor Butch Otter defended Ulukaya and Chobani: "I think his care about his employees, whether they be refugees or they be folks that were born 10 miles from where they're working—I believe his advocacy for that person is no different," Otter told CBS News (2017). "There's nothing wrong with that."

Ulukaya has chosen to stand by his commitment to refugees in general and to Muslim refugees in particular despite the criticism he has received. Ulukaya is reported as saying: "People...hate you for doing something right. There's not much you can do" (CBS News, 2017).

At a time when many people and brands chose to distance themselves from contentious issues, Ulukaya used his billion-dollar-annual-revenue business to both speak to the importance of caring for refugees and to hiring those refugees. He knew he would receive pushback and didn't back down even when he received death threats for proudly supporting people who were being maligned. While there are many ways that Chobani has made a better workplace for religiously diverse people—from raising hourly wages to expanding parental leave—the fact that the organization both hires and vocally fights for the rights and inclusion of refugees, many of whom are Muslim, makes it an exemplar in a divisive time.

Introducing the Kaizen HC Model of Religious Inclusion

Up to this point, we've mostly discussed research, legislation, and definitions of workplace religious diversity, inclusion, and discrimination. Starting with this chapter, we're going to move into discussing the management of workplace religious diversity and inclusion. Each of the chapters in this section will cover:

- Real-world scenarios. We'll explore examples from my own research and professional experience, the news, and the research of my colleagues.
- Context. Each scenario takes place in a specific cultural, legal, political, regional, and national context. Nuance matters in how we consider workplace religious diversity and inclusion and we'll get into the nuance of each situation we discuss to reveal wider trends.
- Lessons. Based on these scenarios and contexts, I will identify important lessons for leaders, employees, organizations, scholars, and politicians. My deepest desire is to provoke thought and help you walk away with practical next steps you can take to make your organization more inclusive.

The goal of each chapter is to help you start to engage in managing religious diversity and inclusion at your organization, whether that be by shifting your own mindset or by supporting employees to express their religion at work.

But how do we know if we're being inclusive of and creating belonging for people of diverse religions? So, often when people ask this question, they are looking for a cut-and-dry answer. They want to hear that if they write a mission statement or hire an IDE consultant or create quiet rooms for prayer and other activities they will have checked religious diversity off their list.

I will provide expert guidance on navigating the challenges of religious diversity and inclusion. As I noted in the introductory chapter, my goal is to provoke thoughtful and meaningful conversations so that you can engage in the work required to assess your organization's commitment to and progress on religious diversity, inclusion, and belonging. To this end, I recommend using two tools: the SOAR framework and a model that I've developed for evaluating the current state of a given organization's religious inclusion practices. My sincere hope is that you will use these tools not as a way to grade your organization, but as a way to celebrate the progress you've made and determine the path before you.

The SOAR (Strengths, Opportunities, Aspirations, and Results) framework is a strategic planning tool developed by Stavros et al. (2003) for implementing systemic change in organizations. As it relates to (religious) IDE, I recommend asking the following questions of your organization:

- *Strengths*—Is there already an established IDE program? Does the organization have IDE as a core value? Is senior leadership committed to IDE? Is there a strong business and moral case for religious IDE? For instance, do key customers, suppliers, and stakeholders take religious diversity seriously?
- *Opportunities*—What are the organization's stakeholders asking for? Are they demanding progress around IDE or a commitment to religious inclusion in the workplace? Can the organization innovate or differentiate itself based on religious IDE in the workplace, marketplace, or society?
- *Aspirations*—What are the organization's values and vision for religious inclusion? Is this truly inclusive or does it prioritize the founders' or leaders' religion over others? Is the IDE vision statement clearly articulated and compelling?
- *Results*—How will the organization know it is succeeding in advancing religious inclusion? What should be the organization's measurable and meaningful outcomes? How should they (voluntarily) obtain and monitor religious diversity and inclusion data? Should they set goals for religious inclusion, and if so, what should they look like? Will targeted goals for religious diversity be useful?

The answers to these questions will help you identify where your organization is, what growth it is ready for next, and where you can go from here. My model gives those answers further structure.

As an IDE expert, I have worked on scholarship around religious diversity; I have worked with clients who seek to make their organizations more inclusive, and over the years of this work, I've identified four levels of religious inclusion in the Kaizen HC Model. Let me begin by offering a brief caveat—these four levels are treated as discrete categories here, but that may not be the case in practice. For example, your organization might have half the attributes of two different levels.

When you read these descriptions, you might be tempted to jump right into the action and change everything in your organization. Before you do, I highly recommend reading each of the chapters contained in Part II, as they illuminate this model even further. No matter where you find yourself on this model, know that you don't need to panic or give up. Organizational culture evolves, and you may be embarking on a new journey to inclusion.

Kaizen HC Model of Religious Inclusion

You might be able to discern from the names and brief descriptions of each level that the ideal level of engagement with inclusion is Level 4: Transformational. In the introduction and in Chapter 2, we discussed the business, moral, and legal cases for this inclusion, and organizations who have reached Level 4 have integrated those cases into the fiber of their organizations (Fig. 4.1).

Let's look at each of these levels a little more in-depth and examine some familiar examples of each.

Organizations that are at Level 1: Avoidance, do not recognize or understand the need for religious diversity in the workplace. They are averse to the legal, business, and moral cases for religious inclusion and belonging at work and in wider society due to any number of reasons from trying to embrace neutrality to a personal bias against one or more religions. Most organizations at this level are homogenous, and employees may belong to only one shared religion that is likely dominant in the wider society. In part due to their relative lack of exposure to people of other religions, these organizations are likely to deny the reality of religious diversity and/or discrimination altogether, avoiding the subject, or doing only the barest minimum required to appear as though they are not engaging in discrimination.

When organizations in Level 1 operate in locations with weak legislative frameworks protecting religious freedom, they may end up promoting only one religion, usually that of the core leadership, above other religions. Preferential treatment and outlooks on this religion can quickly lead to disenfranchisement of people who do not share that religion, whether they be atheists, agnostics, or adherents to another religion. Furthermore, the culture of the organization can become intertwined

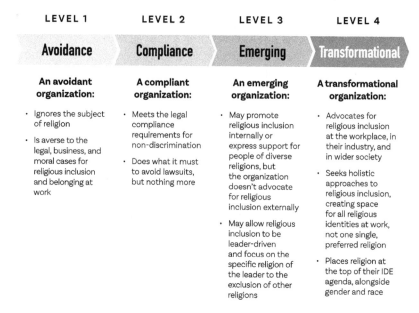

LEVEL 1	LEVEL 2	LEVEL 3	LEVEL 4
Avoidance	**Compliance**	**Emerging**	**Transformational**
An avoidant organization:	A compliant organization:	An emerging organization:	A transformational organization:
• Ignores the subject of religion • Is averse to the legal, business, and moral cases for religious inclusion and belonging at work	• Meets the legal compliance requirements for non-discrimination • Does what it must to avoid lawsuits, but nothing more	• May promote religious inclusion internally or express support for people of diverse religions, but the organization doesn't advocate for religious inclusion externally • May allow religious inclusion to be leader-driven and focus on the specific religion of the leader to the exclusion of other religions	• Advocates for religious inclusion at the workplace, in their industry, and in wider society • Seeks holistic approaches to religious inclusion, creating space for all religious identities at work, not one single, preferred religion • Places religion at the top of their IDE agenda, alongside gender and race

Fig. 4.1   Kaizen HC model of religious inclusion

with the religion of the founders or leaders, and lead to implicit discrimination that may be difficult for members of that religion to recognize.

We have discussed many organizations that are at the "Avoidance" level throughout this book, though perhaps the starkest example would be the case of Kievits Kroon estate's treatment of chef Johanna Mmoledi, which we discuss at length in Chapter 2. The wine estate did not recognize Mmoledi's religion ngoma, wholesale disregarded her healer's note, and subsequently fired her when she missed work to meet with a healer, leading to the South African courts finding Kievits Kroon in the wrong. Kievits Kroon did the bare minimum in the face of Mmoledi's religious request—that is, denying it without even discussing alternatives with the employee. This avoidance and negation led to frustration, headaches, and years of court proceedings, not to mention the damage to Kievits Kroon's reputation. As you can see, "Avoidance" can be a costly level for any organization.

Organizations that reach Level 2: Compliance, have decided they will meet existing legal requirements for the protection of religious freedom but decide to take it no further. They may or may not understand the legal, business, and moral cases for religiously diverse workplaces, but they do all they can to ensure they comply with all laws. These efforts may help them avoid discrimination and protect workers' religious rights, but their goal in regard to religious diversity and inclusion is to avoid lawsuits and the associated costs of them.

Organizations at Level 1 and Level 2 may be indistinguishable from the outside as there is no real commitment to fostering religious diversity, inclusion, and belonging in either, but rather an avoidance of fault and other legal ramifications. In fact, many organizations at "Compliance" have reached this level because they exist in contexts with strong and efficient legislative and institutional frameworks. In other words, in places where there are strong legal frameworks protecting religious freedom, many organizations that might be at Level 1 rise to Level 2 simply because they must.

In Chapter 2, we discussed the existing legal frameworks at play in various nations as well as internationally. Organizations at the "Compliance" level are aware of the legal requirements, and they do what they must to stay compliant. They may, in theory, allow Muslim women to wear that hijab at work, but that theory may not translate to hiring women who wear the hijab in practice. So, just because an organization seems to or does meet the legal requirements to protect the rights of religious people doesn't mean that religious people are actually protected, included, and made to feel as if they belong. For instance, one respondent to my survey, which we'll explore in the next chapter, reported getting the runaround when a potential employer realized she wears a hijab. After completing a very successful phone interview, she arrived for a face-to-face interview only to be told the manager was at lunch. She waited for an hour and was then told the manager was in a car accident while on lunch. She was assured he "would call to reschedule the interview. The call never came. I followed up and was told the manager was on vacation and would set up an interview upon their return. Of course, it never happened." Experiences like these are all too common for religiously diverse workers. It may not always technically be discrimination—or someone who is discriminated against may not be able to *prove* it was discrimination—but people who experience this kind of treatment know when they're being excluded because of their religious identity.

At Level 3: Emerging, organizations understand and respect the legal frameworks for religious diversity and take the conversation further into the area of inclusion. They learn the business and moral cases for religious inclusion and seek to make their workplace safe for people of all religious backgrounds (or none). They may not have a broad understanding of religious inclusion, but they understand that it matters and have a desire to learn more in many cases. These organizations see the benefits of addressing religious diversity and inclusion among their other IDE efforts. Consequently, they may express support for religious inclusion internally and even create internal efforts to support religious inclusion.

That said, these organizations likely do not externally advocate for religious inclusion. They are content with their internal initiatives, which may be leader-driven, and in some cases may focus on the religion of the leader or founder. By extension, other religions may inadvertently be excluded, and employees from diverse religions may feel excluded by organizations at this level. In other words, organizations at Level 3 are not ready to champion religious diversity, inclusion, and belonging—in part because belonging is still an elusive concept to these organizations.

Organizations at Level 3: Emerging recognize the benefits of religious inclusion that we discussed at length in Chapter 3, though they are likely not engaging in activities that foster belonging. At the same time, that internal work doesn't translate to external advocacy. A particularly interesting example of this comes from my own work with clients. At one organization I worked with, a Catholic employee was mocked by a Methodist employee who said, "I better keep my little kids away from you." The Methodist employee was, of course, referencing the horrific abuses of children carried out by some members of the Catholic priesthood. This microaggression made it clear to the Catholic employee that their beliefs and the struggles of their religion weren't valued and in fact, that they were suspect simply because they were Catholic. This kind of guilty by association mentality can quickly erode the efforts of an organization that has reached Level 3, particularly if this mentality is pervasive or there's a pattern across the organization. That's why it's not sufficient to allow for religious expression at work and go no further.

Senior leadership of organizations at Level 3 make religious inclusion an integral and important element of their overall IDE strategy, developing a formal strategy for advancing religious inclusion that clearly articulates the business case for inclusion. Additionally, these organizations have an effective communication plan to address any potential concerns employees may have about bringing religion to the workplace, including clear guidelines and expectations, particularly for the formation of faith-based ERGs, as we'll explore in-depth in Chapter 6.

Furthermore, the example of the microaggression being used against a Catholic employee illuminates that even broad religious groups that we think of as homogenous are, in reality, not. Tensions between subgroups of different religions can arise in the workplace and signal that your inclusion efforts haven't gone far enough.

Level 4: Transformational is the highest in the Kaizen HC Model of Religious Inclusion. Organizations that have reached this level are at the optimal maximization level in terms of religious inclusion and belonging. They have a strong and clear understanding of the legal, business, and moral cases for workplace religious inclusion, and they take a holistic approach to that inclusion. Their aim is to ensure everyone at the organization feels not just safe and included, but as if they belong, inclusive of their religious identity. These organizations do not promote any single religion, but rather create space for all religions to be respected and for dialogue between adherents of different religions, so they can come together to share and exchange their beliefs, commonalities, and differences.

Organizations at Level 4 integrate religion into their diversity, equity, and inclusion initiatives alongside gender and race. It is not an afterthought or an add-on, but rather a basic component of how people are cared for at the organization. Finally, organizations at Level 4 keep abreast with current global religious diversity issues and practices, to some degree.

At this level, it is not only the leaders who drive religious inclusion. There is a general sense in the organization that everyone is responsible for creating a sense of belonging for a religiously diverse workforce. The leaders and organization do not prefer a single religious group or denomination, and they make deliberate efforts to make people of all faiths feel welcome. Religious inclusion is a fundamental part of the IDE strategy for Level 4 organizations, and they invest in employee resource groups (ERGs), which they use as a lever to attract, retain, and engage a religiously diverse workforce.

This chapter opened with a great example of an organization at Level 4: Transformational. Chobani embodies the best of what we can do to create inclusion for religious people at work and beyond. While we focused on how Ulukaya responded to criticisms in the lead up to the

2016 U.S. presidential election, Chobani was active around immigration and refugees before that time.

In his address to Davos and an early-2016 op-ed, Ulukaya took a pro-refugee stance as a person and as a business leader. He encouraged businesses to capitalize on the refugee crisis to infuse their organizations with new energy and workers who are loyal and hardworking. Not only did Ulukaya mention the moral obligation to address the worst humanitarian crisis since World War II, but he also outlined the contributions of many refugees to societies in the West. And, in 2017, when the Trump administration announced a travel ban on seven Muslim-majority countries, Ulukaya released an internal memo addressing the ban. In it, he wrote: "This is very personal for me. As an immigrant who came to this country looking for opportunity, it's very difficult to think about and imagine what millions of people around the world must be feeling right now" (Wiener-Bronner & Alesci, 2017).

You can see that Ulukaya takes measures to be clear both externally and internally that refugees belong in the U.S. and they belong at Chobani. Now, Chobani provides an interesting example because it's not as if they talk exclusively about Muslims and creating inclusion for Muslim people. However, given that many of the refugees Chobani has hired are from Muslim countries, all of the advocacy work being done has been inclusive of Muslims. You might expect that reaching Level 4 requires having a big banner that says all religions welcome here hanging in your front office. In reality, religious inclusion and belonging can take on many different faces, as you've seen with Chobani.

By this point, you realize that religious diversity, inclusion, and belonging have many facets and intricacies that can make the conversation challenging. There are many variables between and within religious groups, and there are many different contexts in which these religions operate. That's why I've included so many real-world examples in this book: I want you to know the facts that I'm working with, see how I've analyzed and evaluated the situation, and observe how I've come to my own conclusion about how inclusive or not an organization is.

It is challenging to conduct an objective analysis—believe me, I've seen plenty of organizations struggle with this process and, in some cases, give up. The Kaizen HC Model for Religious Inclusion is my effort to reveal some of my thought processes to you, so that you can begin to evaluate your own organization and how inclusive it is—not as the final word on your organization's inclusion efforts, but rather, as a foundation from which to build your strategies for religious inclusion.

No matter where you find your organization in this model, I want to encourage you to not look at this as a static position; inclusion is an evolving process. Any organization can move between levels, and any organization can reach Level 4. At the same time, organizations that find themselves in Level 4 can still benefit from a periodic analysis of their religious inclusion level to ensure they're always responsive to a changing climate. My goal is not for you to use this as a checklist that you go through once, but rather to use this model as continual guidance so you can assess and increase the level of religious inclusion and belonging at your organization.

More than anything, I want this model to be useful to you. As you read through this next part of the book, think about your organization, and how it might be similar or different from the various examples and contexts we'll be exploring. These scenarios will help you develop your own understanding of the model, see how other organizations strive for inclusion and belonging (or don't), and hopefully, identify your own opportunities for growth.

References

CBS News (2017, April 6). *Chobani founder stands by hiring refugees.* https://www.cbsnews.com/news/chobani-founder-stands-by-hiring-refugees/

Pathak, S. (2016, November 3). With founder under fire for employing refugees, Chobani gets brand boost from supportive customers. *Digiday.* https://digiday.com/marketing/chobani-gets-brand-boost-supportive-customers/

Stavros, J. M., Cooperrider, D., & Kelley, L. (2003). Strategic inquiry—Appreciative intent: Inspiration to SOAR. *AI Practitioner,* 2–19. https://appreciativeinquiry.champlain.edu/educational-material/strategic-inquiry-appreciative-intent-inspiration-to-soar/

Ulukaya, H. (2016, January 20). Opinion: Big business must 'hack' refugee crisis. *CNNMoney.* https://money.cnn.com/2016/01/20/news/refugees-business-davos-opinion/

Wiener-Bronner, D., & Alesci, C. (2017, January 30). Chobani CEO finds Trump's travel ban 'personal for me.' *CNNMoney.* https://money.cnn.com/2017/01/30/news/chobani-response-travel-ban/index.html

Wearing the Hijab and Experiences of Discrimination in the U.S. Workplace

Abstract Stigmatization of the hijab or headscarf is a common xenophobic reaction in the workplace. From America to France, and Germany
to India, Muslim women who wear the hijab face prejudice and bigotry.
This chapter offers empirical evidence of wide-spread discrimination
against hijab-wearing Muslim women in the U.S., and how this and other
forms of religious discrimination have increased since the September 11,
2001 attacks. The study serves as an example of how the interplay of
the legal protections, motivational factors, organizational standards, and
social barriers informs options of religious discrimination or inclusion in
the workplace

Keywords Hijab · Religious garb and grooming · Muslim women ·
Religious discrimination · Workplace stigma

The world was forever changed on September 11, 2001, when thousands
of people lost their lives in a terror attack in the U.S. Despite the loca-
tion of the attack itself, the aftermath of these heinous events has rippled
throughout the world. These attacks prompted major changes culturally
and politically that have far-reaching consequences. If you've flown before
and after that time, you know that airplane travel has become much more

© The Author(s), under exclusive license to Springer Nature   61
Switzerland AG 2022
E. Hasan, *Embracing Workplace Religious Diversity and Inclusion*,
Palgrave Studies in Equity, Diversity, Inclusion, and Indigenization
in Business, https://doi.org/10.1007/978-3-030-89773-4_5

regulated and restricted. Nations including the U.S. have also used the terror attacks to justify surveillance laws like the Patriot Act. Though we have all been impacted by such changes, religious minorities including Muslims and Sikhs have experienced much worse.

In the aftermath of the 9/11 attacks, for instance, according to the American Civil Liberties Union (ACLU, 2008), Muslim women who wear the hijab have been fired from jobs, harassed, and denied access to public places both in the U.S. and around the world. This discrimination is often referred to as hijabophobia; in recent years, perceived and documented workplace discrimination toward Muslims, including Muslim women who wear the hijab, have been increasing. According to research conducted by the Pew Research Center in 2020, between 2016 and 2018, Muslim women faced discrimination for wearing head coverings in forty-two of the fifty-six countries studied in Europe, Americas, Asia–Pacific, Sub-Saharan Africa, the Middle East, and North Africa regions.

In the U.S., 3.45 million Muslims make up 1.1% of the population (Mohamed, 2018). This number may appear insignificant, but the Muslim population in the U.S. is fast growing, and it is projected to be about 8.1 million by 2050 (Mohamed, 2018). Islam is also the fastest-growing religion in the world and expanding to many countries. As the number of people who identify as Muslims continues to increase, hijab wearing women are sure to also become more numerous. The religious discrimination faced by this population who already make up a substantial part of our society, the market, and the workplace cannot be ignored.

What Is the Hijab, and Why Does It Matter?

To explore the unique experiences of Muslim women who wear the hijab, we must share a basic understanding of the hijab and its religious significance. The hijab, known as *hijaba* in the Arabic language, means to cover or conceal (Aslam, 2011; Ghumman & Ryan, 2013). It can also refer to several different things, including a woman covering her body from neck to ankle or, as it often does in the Western culture, it could mean simply wearing a headscarf (Ghumman & Ryan, 2013). In the simplest definition, a hijab is a headscarf worn by Muslim women, who are sometimes referred to as hijabis (Ghumman & Ryan, 2013). The hijab is one of the most visible artifacts of religious expression for Muslim women (Ali et al., 2015).

While it is impractical to explore the varied religious and legal inter-pretations of the hijab, as many texts have been dedicated to this task, it is safe to say the hijab is deeply rooted in the religion of Islam and its Holy Book, the Quran (Aslam, 2011; Robinson et al., 2012; Tariq-Munir, 2014). Among Muslims there is a good deal of debate as to whether it is a requirement for Muslim women to wear the hijab (Ghumman & Ryan, 2013). Some opponents of the hijab argue that it is a cultural phenomenon rather than a religious requirement (Ghumman & Ryan, 2013). Others argue that the hijab is emblematic of social hierarchies and male domination and is merely a proliferation of mediocrity and servility that seeks to oppress Muslim women (Ghumman & Ryan, 2013; Read & Bartkowski, 2000). Others argue that the Quran tangentially mentions the veil but does not explicitly mandate that women should wear it (Paulose, 2015; Read & Bartkowski, 2000).

Whether or not the hijab is a religious requirement, many Muslim women choose to wear it of their own will for both religious and symbolic purposes (Aslam, 2011; Tariq-Munir, 2014). So, many Muslim women who wear the hijab are not forced or mandated to do so (Tariq-Munir, 2014), and view it as a religious symbol that helps define identity and exudes empowerment (Ali et al., 2015). Women wear the head-scarf for various reasons including resisting sexual objectification, having greater control over their bodies, and preserving intimate relationships (Droogsma, 2007). Several women have also stated that they wear the hijab because of the identity it provides for Muslim women, and the friendships that are formed with fellow hijab-wearing women (Read & Bartkowski, 2000). The hijab is worn by some due to parental expecta-tions and peer pressure, and wearing the hijab is also sometimes viewed as a litmus test as to whether a woman is a good Muslim or not. To many Muslim women, the hijab is viewed as a symbol of freedom and a distin-guished social identity, and it is worn by many kinds of women including the highly educated (Kulenović, 2006). It is devastating that a symbol of strength and empowerment is so often used as justification to belittle and demean Muslim women, and the sad truth is that Muslim women who wear the hijab experience discrimination and exclusion on several levels in the workplace.

THE PERVASIVENESS OF WORKPLACE DISCRIMINATION AGAINST HIJAB-WEARING MUSLIM WOMEN

The right of Muslim women to wear the hijab in public and in the workplace is protected by the First and Fourteenth Amendments of the U.S. Constitution (Constitution Annotated, n.d.a; Constitution Annotated, n.d.b) and by Title VII of the Civil Rights Act of 1964. Despite constitutional and statutory protections, in the year following 9/11 the average number of complaints filed with the EEOC by Muslims in the workforce increased by 172% (2016), and many of those complaints were filed by Muslim women who wear the hijab (Moore, 2007). In 2015, the EEOC reported that workplace discrimination toward Muslims was still on average 168% higher than it was prior to 9/11 (2016).

The Council on American-Islamic Relations (CAIR), an organization dedicated to defending the civil rights and liberties of Muslims in America, provides free legal services to those who have been subject to anti-Muslim discrimination. In 2020, CAIR received over 6,000 complaints; employment discrimination made up 57% of the total complaints received (CAIR, 2021). That year, CAIR branches throughout the U.S. filed wrongful termination and discrimination cases, ranging from hostile work environments to harassment. In many cases, this harassment and discrimination was targeted at Muslim women who wear the hijab (CAIR, 2021).

In many of these cases, there may be specific data about the experiences of Muslims, but it is rare to have much data on the experiences of Muslim women who wear the hijab. That's why I conducted an online survey of 229 Muslim women who wear the hijab as part of the research for my dissertation at USC. I wanted to explore the extent to which Muslim women who wear the hijab experience discrimination in the workplace. The results are illuminating:

Almost 67% of respondents strongly agreed or agreed that there was a negative stereotype of women who wear the hijab in the workplace. Around 17% of respondents believed wearing the hijab resulted in an instance when they were terminated from a job.

Of the Muslim women surveyed, 53% felt less confident about obtaining a job when wearing the hijab while 53% believed that wearing the hijab resulted in an instance when they did not obtain a job. In fact, one respondent shared the following experience:

I completed a six-month internship in Texas in my field and was told that
if I did well I may be offered a job. Instead, I was told, 'sorry but (our
organization) is just not ready for a Muslim'.

Another respondent was told by a recruiter she wouldn't be able to get
a job in the business field despite her qualifications and that she should
pursue a career in medicine instead.

Almost 40%—38.2% to be exact—of respondents reported witnessing
other women being discriminated against in the workplace because of
their hijab. A majority—70%—agreed that there is a negative stereotyping
of women who wear the hijab in the workplace while 59.6% agreed to the
possibility of stereotyping of hijab-wearing women affecting their confidence. One respondent said, "I know that my hijab will always be the first
thing they consider, and not my qualifications."

Interestingly, most respondents (74.7%) either strongly agreed or
agreed that their employers were accepting of their hijab, and 68.2% either
strongly agreed or agreed that their employer did enough to protect their
religious rights in the workplace.

Additionally, several prominent cases of workplace discrimination
toward women who wear the hijab have also been documented.

- In 2001, Alamo Rent-A-Car terminated the job of Bilan Nur for
  refusing to remove her hijab even though she was formerly allowed
  to wear the hijab (Aslam, 2011; Marcum & Perry, 2010).
- In 2008, Abercrombie & Fitch refused to hire Halla Banafa because
  of her hijab; the company's store manager wrote "not Abercrombie
  look" on Banafa's interview form when meeting with her (Aslam,
  2011). In another case involving Abercrombie & Fitch, the company
  refused to hire Samantha Elauf because her hijab violated the company's look policy, and she was later awarded $25,670 in damages
  (ACLU, 2008; Aslam, 2011).
- In 2010, Disney, citing its look policy, terminated the appointment
  of Imane Boudlal because of her refusal to wear an alternative hat in
  lieu of her hijab (ACLU, 2012; Robinson et al., 2012).
- In 2012, the Morningside House of Ellicott City located in Mary-
  land was required to pay $25,000 dollars for refusing to hire
  Khadijah Salim because she declined to remove her hijab, and the
  company was also required to post a notice of its commitment to

having a work environment free of religious discrimination (EEOC, 2012).

- In 2016, Fair Oaks Dental Care located in Fairfax, Virginia, citing its preference to maintain a religiously neutral work environment to not offend patients, allegedly terminated the job of Najaf Khan for her refusal to remove her hijab (CAIR, 2016; Stone, 2016).
- In 2021, an assistant manager at a Chipotle Mexican Grill in Kansas allegedly demanded that a Muslim woman remove her hijab. He also allegedly physically removed the hijab from her head while she was working. The worker ultimately resigned, and the assistant manager was dismissed by Chipotle (Clarey, 2021).

Paired with research, these cases, and indeed several others, suggest that discrimination faced by Muslim women who wear the hijab is still a challenge.

Unfortunately, weak or nonexistent legal and institutional frameworks do not fully address workplace religious discrimination in many countries, a clear call for more robust and lasting solutions. Hijab-wearing Muslim women and persons who can potentially face religious discrimination in the workplace need to have knowledge of the legal protections and resources available to them to address workplace religious discrimination. The survey I conducted supports this sentiment. The data demonstrates that participants had good factual understanding of their rights and the resources available, while 68.5% of participants either strongly disagreed or disagreed about knowing the process of filing an EEOC complaint.

The discrimination Muslim women face keeps them from fully engaging in the workplace. We must address this discrimination and barriers to inclusion both for the benefit of all workers and organizations.

Workplace Religious Discrimination Against Muslim Women, and Barriers to Inclusion

To identify the barriers and influences of workplace religious discrimination, let's examine four concepts. Three are drawn from Clark and Estes (2008)'s gap analysis framework, which identifies knowledge and skills, motivation, and organizational barriers to addressing religious discrimination in the workplace. These three broad categories interact to influence the performance goals of individuals and businesses. Effective solutions to eliminating performance gaps can be achieved by individuals and businesses after careful analyses of the factors within each of these three categories. For our purposes, I've identified a fourth category: social barriers, which also merits close consideration alongside organizational barriers.

Knowledge

Due to the pervasiveness of discrimination against hijab-wearing Muslim women and workplace religious discrimination generally, it is imperative for workers to have knowledge of the legal protections that address religious discrimination in the workplace. As already suggested by Mujtaba and Cavico (2012), educating the workforce is a critical factor in solving religious problems in the workplace.

Knowledge can be divided into four categories—factual, conceptual, procedural, and metacognitive (Krathwohl, 2002; Rueda, 2011). I focus only on factual knowledge and procedural knowledge because they are most relevant to the protection of workers against religious discrimination in the workplace. The factual knowledge workers require is indicative of knowing the constitutional rights, statutory rights, and resources (e.g., the EEOC in the U.S.) that protect religious rights in the workplace. With respect to workplace religious discrimination, procedural knowledge pertains to the steps required to file a religion-based discrimination complaint with an employer's HR department or with the local, regional, or national authority in one's country.

Many employees lack the knowledge of employment laws and constitutional and statutory laws that protect them from religious discrimination in the workplace. They also are not aware of the necessary procedures and steps to take in case of instances of discrimination in the workplace. In one study, 2,400 participants were asked to confirm whether a series of actions by employers were legal or illegal. In that study, nearly 74% of the participants incorrectly identified legal actions by employers to be illegal, roughly 78% were able to identify which actions were unlawful, and approximately 83% incorrectly answered that it was illegal to terminate an employee for no reason as provided by the employment-at-will rule (Freeman & Rogers as cited by Eliasoph, 2008).

My own survey also yielded interesting results. Fifty-two percent of the women agreed that their employer's HR department is equipped to handle religious discrimination in the workplace, and 53.8% agreed that they felt comfortable with reporting religious discrimination to that department. At the same time, most participants either strongly agreed or agreed (89.6%) to knowing their constitutional and statutory rights and the resources available to address religious discrimination in the workplace (68.1%). Despite these numbers, the data suggested that participants did not have a good procedural understanding of how to file an EEOC complaint. Sixty-eight percent of the participants either strongly disagreed or disagreed with knowing the process of filing an EEOC complaint.

Motivation

Numerous definitions of motivation have been offered by scholars and practitioners. According to Mayer (2011), "motivation is an internal state that initiates and maintains goal directed behavior," (p. 39) and it is personal, activating, energizing, and directed. Clark and Estes (2008) defined motivation as something that "gets us going, keeps us moving, and tells us how much effort to spend on a task." Motivation is influenced by internal and external factors (Schunk et al. as cited by Rueda, 2011).

One external motivation factor that relates to workplace religious discrimination is stereotype threat. Stereotype threat describes an individual's tendency to inadvertently validate a stereotype of a group they are associated with while attempting to accomplish a goal (Steele & Aronson, 1995). When performing a task, individuals associated with stigmatized groups exhibit a fear of conforming to the negative stereotypes related to their groups, thus inadvertently causing them to underperform on those tasks (Ghumman & Jackson, 2010). The individual experiencing group-related stereotyping does not have to believe that a stereotype is true. However, the mere threat that a stereotype exists can cause the individual to validate that stereotype (Steele & Aronson, 1995).

In assessing how wearing the hijab impacted the employability of Muslim women, Pasha-Zaidi et al. (2014) hypothesized that religious attire activates stereotype threat, specifically that Muslim women who wear the hijab will be viewed less favorably for employment. In this study, participants were asked to view two photographs of the same woman with and without the hijab and were asked the likelihood of the woman obtaining a position as a doctor, laundry worker, graphic designer, or personal household cook. The study found that the participants in the U.S., both hijab-wearing and non-hijab-wearing, rated non-hijab-wearing women higher for employability.

Therefore, the despondency that stereotype threat engenders could cause Muslim women who wear the hijab to believe that they cannot be successful no matter what they do, thus discouraging them from actively pursuing a goal, persisting through stereotypes, or investing enough mental effort.

There are two key internal motivation factors of particular relevance to women wearing a hijab: self-efficacy and attribution. Self-efficacy postulates that an individual's motivation to accomplish a task or goal is influenced by the belief in their ability to produce the desired outcome (Bandura, 1991). Individuals with high self-efficacy are more likely to ascribe their failure to their lack of effort, whereas people with low self-efficacy will attribute their failure to a lack of ability (Bandura, 1991). Moreover, highly self-efficacious individuals experience joy or happiness when confronted with a difficult task while individuals with low self-efficacy exhibit despondent behaviors.

Self-efficacy may be diminished in Muslim women who wear the hijab, as evidenced by several studies. Hijab-wearing women have lower expectations for their job prospects than non-hijab-wearing women, regardless of occupation (Ghumman & Jackson, 2010). In a survey of 219 Muslim women, 30% of the Muslim women who wear the hijab stated that they were concerned about applying for jobs, 22% stated that they were denied employment, and 63% said they were aware of times that other hijab-wearing women were denied employment (Ghumman & Jackson, 2010; University of Hawaii at Manoa, 2010).

Meanwhile, attribution is what an individual believes to be the cause of success or failure in a given situation (Anderman & Anderman, 2006; Rueda, 2011). A comparison of hijab-wearing and non-hijab-wearing women showed that there is a negative correlation between wearing the hijab and receiving permission to complete a job application, receiving a job call-back, and the applicant's expectation of receiving a job offer (Ghumman & Ryan, 2013). These negative correlations are not arbitrary.

An earlier study by King and Ahmad (2010) also found that women in Muslim attire who do not attempt to counteract the stereotypes of Muslims are more likely to face a challenge finding a job, and they had experienced more negative interactions when wearing religious attire than when they did not. Women who wear the hijab are also more likely to face higher rejection rates when applying for jobs, regardless of their level of education (Unkelbach et al., 2010).

Organizational and Social

An organization's culture, inadequate resources, and flawed policies and procedures can be barriers to employees accomplishing their goals (Clark & Estes, 2008). Also, there are several social factors outside of the organization that act as barriers and influence discrimination against hijab-wearing women, including political, legal, and cultural environments these hijab-wearing women, workers, and employers operate in. Both internal organizational and wider social barriers act jointly as they are interrelated. Furthermore, both contribute to cultural norms, another facet than can serve as a barrier or influence to achieving an individual's goals. In Chapters 2 and 3 we discussed political and legal environments and how they are shifting due to emerging global trends; what remains is to discuss culture, and how it influences hijab-wearing women's experiences in the workplace.

Schein (2004) defined culture as "shared basic assumptions that was learned by a group as it solved its problems...that has worked well enough to be taught to new members as the correct way to perceive, think, and feel in relation to those problems" (p. 18). According to Clark and Estes (2008), culture is a multi-dimensional and dynamic construct that is both conscious and unconscious and serves as a conduit for describing the values, goals, beliefs, and processes learned by people over time. Gallimore and Goldenberg (2001) bifurcate culture into two categories: cultural models and cultural settings. Cultural models are taken-for-granted norms that exist within organizations, societies, or individuals, and serve as an invisible toolkit on how to perceive or approach situations (Gallimore & Goldenberg, 2001; Rueda, 2011). Cultural settings are where "people come together to carry out a joint activity that accomplishes something they value (Gallimore & Goldenberg, 2001). Therefore, cultural settings are visible, and they are the social contexts in which cultural models are created and acted out, such as workplaces or classroom settings (Rueda, 2011). Both cultural models and cultural settings can be seen as influences or barriers to accomplishing a goal (Clark & Estes, 2008).

Women who wear the hijab in the U.S. encounter two major cultural models that may serve as barriers to their ability to protect themselves from workplace religious discrimination: the American cultural model and the hijab cultural model. The American cultural model espouses the need for a separation of church and state (Inglehart & Norris, 2002). Values such as equality, liberty, and individualism are at the core of American culture (Williams & Vashi, 2007). The hijab, then, can be seen as incongruent with the American culture because it is viewed as a symbol of inequality and oppression of Muslim women (Droogsma, 2007) and as an indicator of women being inferior to men (Cole & Ahmadi, 2003). Therefore, many people view wearing the hijab as illogical, conflating the experiences of Muslim women in the U.S. with those of women being treated unfairly in several Muslim countries (Williams & Vashi, 2007).

As we discussed at the beginning of this chapter, the hijab cultural model espouses the belief that the hijab represents empowerment, their commitment to Islam, and the freedom to choose their own identity. Williams and Vashi (2007) suggest that wearing the hijab allows women to create a cultural space for themselves, as part of their American culture, and allows them to negotiate their identities as Muslims and Americans and to be a part of both worlds. It has also been suggested that Muslim women wear the hijab as a form of resistance to the West's disposition toward their religion and culture (Hamadan as cited in Ali et al., 2015). As such, when juxtaposing the American cultural model with the hijab cultural model, a natural dissonance emerges that leaves hijab-wearing women attempting to figure out what the appropriate practices are in certain situations or settings, for example in the workplace (Williams & Vashi, 2007). Meanwhile, the workplace cultural setting has been a major influence on the ability of hijab-wearing women to protect themselves against workplace religious discrimination (ACLU, 2008).

Knowledge, motivation, organization, and social barriers and influences do not operate independently but are actually interrelated. As such, for Muslim women who wear the hijab, and by extension all workers who may experience workplace religious discrimination, overcoming knowledge, motivation, organizational, and social factors is of the utmost importance.

Workplace religious discrimination is fueled by these interconnected factors. When we ensure Muslim women who wear the hijab and all workers who might experience workplace discrimination have the knowledge, motivation, and organizational and social support to succeed, we not only make the workplace better for all workers but also increase the performance of individuals and teams.

Organizations, leaders, and members of society, in general, have much they can take away from my research on the experiences of Muslim women who wear the hijab (Hasan, 2018). From the importance of education around the EEOC and religious discrimination to being able to understand and identify how stereotype threat limits the motivation and success of religiously diverse employees, we can create cultural settings that are safe for religiously diverse people who come with their unique cultural models. And when we identify the barriers that come from our own cultural models, our organizations, and our societies, we can find ways not just to overcome those barriers, but to address the source of the problem so we can make lasting change. It's an ambitious goal, and that's why every chapter in this section is dedicated to helping you lay the foundation for that change.

Assessing the Level of Religious Inclusion Among U.S. Employers

Throughout this chapter, we've explored case after case of workplace religious discrimination against Muslim women who wear the hijab. Unfortunately, this reality is reflected in the responses to my survey of Muslim women who have also experienced a range of discriminatory behaviors.

In each example, the details may vary, but it's safe to say that at the time of the various events the organizations engaging in discrimination were at Level 1: Avoidance. Many court cases are still being litigated, of course, but one might assume that with such high-profile incidents the organizations in question might be motivated to avoid further legal consequences by moving to Level 2: Compliance. By and large, that does not seem to be the case, yet.

Organizations that desire to reach Level 2: Compliance would be wise to conduct an audit of their policies, both in terms of dress code and otherwise, to ensure they are in alignment with legal requirements, the revised guidance on workplace religious discrimination from the EEOC mentioned in Chapter 2, and various court rulings as precedent is established. Not only is it the best way to avoid costly litigation costs, but it's also the first step toward creating a better workplace for Muslim women who wear the hijab and other religiously diverse employees. 9/11 changed the way we live and work in the U.S. and around the world—and for Muslims in the U.S. and Muslim women who wear the hijab in particular, that change has manifested in the form of rampant discrimination. It's our job as policymakers, academicians, and citizens to fight this discrimination for the betterment of us all.

Just fighting discrimination isn't enough. We don't want to settle for tolerance or mere acceptance in our workplaces, but rather, we should be working to create greater inclusion and belonging for religious people at work. In the next chapter, we'll explore one helpful tool for creating inclusion and belonging: ERGs.

REFERENCES

ACLU. (2012). Muslim former employee sues Disney for discrimination. *American Civil Liberties Union*. https://www.aclusocal.org/muslim-former-employee-sues-disney/
ACLU. (2008). Discrimination against Muslim women. *American Civil Liberties Union*. https://www.aclu.org/other/discrimination-against-muslim-women-fact-sheet
Ali, S. R., Yamada, T., & Mahmood, A. (2015). Relationships of the practice of hijab, workplace discrimination, social class, job stress, and job satisfaction among Muslim American women. *Journal of Employment Counseling, 52*(4), 146–157. https://doi.org/10.1002/joec.12020
Anderman, E., & Anderman, L. (2006). *Attributions*. http://www.education.com/reference/article/attribution-theory/
Aslam, S. (2011). Hijab in the workplace: Why title VII does not adequately protect employees from discrimination on the basis of religious dress and appearance. *UMKC Law Review, 80*(1), 221.
Bandura, A. (1991). Social cognitive theory of self-regulation. *Organizational Behavior and Human Decision Processes, 50*(2), 248–287. https://doi.org/10.1016/0749-5978(91)90022-L
Clarey, K. (2021, September 14). Muslim Chipotle worker files EEOC complaint alleging assistant manager yanked hijab. *Restaurant Dive*. https://www.restaurantdive.com/news/muslim-chipotle-worker-files-eeoc-complaint-alleging-assistant-manager-yank/606529/
Clark, R. E., & Estes, F. (2008). *Turning research into results: A guide to selecting the right performance solutions*. Information Age Publishing.
Cole, D., & Ahmadi, S. (2003). Perspectives and experiences of Muslim women who veil on college campuses. *Journal of College Student Development, 44*(1), 47–66.
CAIR (Council on American-Islamic Relations). (2016, August 3). *CAIR seeks reinstatement of Va. Muslim woman fired over hijab*. https://www.cair.com/press_releases/cair-seeks-reinstatement-of-va-muslim-woman-fired-over-hijab/
CAIR (Council on American-Islamic Relations). (2021). *Resilience in the face of hate*. https://www.cair.com/wp-content/uploads/2021/04/CAIRReport.pdf

Constitution Annotated. (n.d.a). *First Amendment: Freedom of religion, speech, press, assembly, and petition.* https://constitution.congress.gov/browse/amendment-1/

Constitution Annotated. (n.d.b). *Fourteenth Amendment: Citizenship, equal protection, and other Post-Civil War provisions.* https://constitution.congress.gov/browse/amendment-14/

Droogsma, R. A. (2007). Redefining hijab: American Muslim women's standpoints on veiling. *Journal of Applied Communication Research, 35*(3), 294–319.

EEOC. (n.d.). *Title VII of the Civil Rights Act of 1964.* https://www.eeoc.gov/statutes/title-vii-civil-rights-act-1964#:~:text=Title%20VII%20prohibits%20employment%20discrimination,religion%2C%20sex%20and%20national%20origin

EEOC. (2012). *Morningside House of Ellicott City to pay $25,000 for religious discrimination.* https://www.eeoc.gov/newsroom/morningside-house-ellicott-city-pay-25000-religious-discrimination

EEOC. (2016). *Charges filed on the basis of religion - Muslim or national origin - middle eastern FY 1995-FY 2015.* https://www.eeoc.gov/eeoc/statistics/enforcement/religion_muslim_origin_middle_eastern.cfm

Eliasoph, I. (2008). Know your (lack of) rights: Reexamining the causes and effects of phantom employment rights. *Employee Rights and Employment Policy Journal, 12*(2), 197–232.

Gallimore, R., & Goldenberg, C. (2001). Analyzing cultural models and settings to connect minority achievement and school improvement research. *Educational Psychologist, 36*(1), 45–56. https://doi.org/10.1207/S15326985EP3601_5

Ghumman, S., & Jackson, L. (2010). The downside of religious attire: The Muslim headscarf and expectations of obtaining employment. *Journal of Organizational Behavior, 31*(1), 4–23.

Ghumman, S., & Ryan, A. M. (2013). Not welcome here: Discrimination towards women who wear the Muslim headscarf. *Human Relations, 66*(5), 671–698. https://doi.org/10.1177/0018726712469540

Hasan, E. (2018). *Workplace religious discrimination toward Muslim women who wear the hijab* [Ed. D Dissertation, University of Southern California].

Inglehart, R., & Norris, P. (2002). Islamic culture and democracy: Testing the 'clash of civilizations' thesis. *Comparative Sociology, 1*(3–4), 235–263. https://doi.org/10.1163/156913302100418592

King, E. B., & Ahmad, A. S. (2010). An experimental field study of interpersonal discrimination toward Muslim job applicants. *Personnel Psychology, 63*(4), 881–906.

Krathwohl, D. R. (2002). A revision of Bloom's taxonomy: An overview. *Theory into Practice, 41*(4), 212–218. https://doi.org/10.1207/s15430421 tip4104_2

Kulenović, T. (2006). A veil (hijab) as a public symbol of a Muslim woman modern identity. *Collegium Antropologicum, 30*(4), 713–718.

Marcum, T., & Perry, S. J. (2010). Dressed for success: Can a claim of religious discrimination be successful? *Labor Law Journal, 61*(4), 184.

Mayer, R. E. (2011). *Applying the science of learning*. Pearson.

Mohamed, B. (2018). New estimates show U.S. Muslim population continues to grow. *Pew Research Center*. https://www.pewresearch.org/fact-tank/2018/01/03/new-estimates-show-u-s-muslim-population-continues-to-grow/

Moore, K. M. (2007). Visible through the veil: The regulation of Islam in American law. *Sociology of Religion, 68*(3), 237–251. https://doi.org/10.1093/soc rel/68.3.237

Mujtaba, B. G., & Cavico, F. J. (2012). Discriminatory practices against Muslims in the American workplace. *Journal of Leadership, Accountability and Ethics, 9*(1), 98.

Pasha-Zaidi, N., Masson, T., & Pennington, M. N. (2014). Can I get a job if I wear hijab? An exploratory study of the perceptions of South Asian Muslim women in the US and the UAE. *International Journal of Research Studies in Psychology, 3*(1). https://doi.org/10.5861/ijrsp.2013.357

Paulose, R. K. (2015). Is an employer liable under Title VII of the Civil Rights Act only if the employer has actual knowledge of the need for a religious accommodation based on direct notice from an applicant or employee? *Preview of United States Supreme Court Cases, 42*(5), 179–183.

Pew Research Center. (2020). *Women in many countries face harassment for clothing deemed too religious – or too secular*. https://www.pewresearch.org/fact-tank/2020/12/16/women-in-many-countries-face-harassment-for-clo thing-deemed-too-religious-or-too-secular/

Read, J. G., & Bartkowski, J. P. (2000). To veil or not to veil? A case study of identity negotiation among Muslim women in Austin, Texas. *Gender & Society, 14*(3), 395–417. https://doi.org/10.1177/089124300014003003

Robinson, R. K., Franklin, G. M., & Hamilton, R. H. (2012). The hijab and the kufi: Employer rights to convey their business image versus employee rights to religious expression. *Southern Law Journal, 22*(1), 79.

Rueda, R. (2011). *The 3 dimensions of improving student performance*. Teachers College Press.

Schein, E. H. (2004). *Organizational culture and leadership* (3rd ed.). Jossey-Bass.

Steele, C. M., & Aronson, J. (1995). Stereotype threat and the intellectual test performance of African Americans. *Journal of Personality and Social Psychology, 69*(5), 797–811. https://doi.org/10.1037/0022-3514.69.5.797

Stone, S. (2016, August 3). *Virginia woman says she was fired for wearing hijab [video]*. https://www.nbcwashington.com/news/local/Virginia-Woman-Says-She-Was-Fired-for-Wearing-Hijab-389134252.html

Tariq-Munir, E. (2014). *The dynamics of wearing hijab for Muslim American women in the United States* [Master's thesis, Iowa State University). https://dr.lib.iastate.edu/server/api/core/bitstreams/549fcfd3-e7e4-4cfe-a6d8-a6e93aa25021/content

Unkelbach, C., Schneider, H., Gode, K., & Senft, M. (2010). A turban effect, too: Selection biases against women wearing Muslim headscarves. *Social Psychological and Personality Science, 1*(4), 378–383.

University of Hawaii at Manoa. (2010). *Muslim women who wear headscarves face workplace discrimination in US: Study*. http://phys.org/news/2010-09-muslim-women-headscarves-workplace-discrimination.html

Williams, R. H., & Vashi, G. (2007). 'Hijab' and American Muslim women: Creating the space for autonomous selves. *Sociology of Religion, 68*(3), 269–287. https://doi.org/10.1093/socrel/68.3.269

CHAPTER 6

Praying for Faith-Based Employee Resource Groups in America

Abstract In an increasingly religiously diverse society and workplace, fostering a sense of belonging among employees must be an organizational priority. Many forward-thinking organizations are taking this challenge seriously, establishing faith-based employee resource groups (ERGs). The chapter provides practical approaches to leveraging ERGs to advance religious inclusion. Three models of ERGs—faith-specific, interfaith, and interfaith network—and examples of how ERGs are structured are described in real-life case studies (Salesforce and American Express). The CFC case study delves into the dilemmas and decision-making processes of an American organization launching its faith-based ERG.

Keywords Employee resource groups · Faith-based groups · Belonging · Identity covering · Religious diversity

Recently, a Chief Human Resource Officer we'll call Kathy nervously prepared for her monthly meeting with her supervisor and the company's CEO, Hugh. For the last year, she had been working for Cardinal Forest Company (CFC), a manufacturer of greeting cards, gift wrap, and holiday gifts, after working for one of CFC's competitors, Mulberry Cards, for

© The Author(s), under exclusive license to Springer Nature   77
Switzerland AG 2022
E. Hasan, *Embracing Workplace Religious Diversity and Inclusion*,
Palgrave Studies in Equity, Diversity, Inclusion, and Indigenization
in Business, https://doi.org/10.1007/978-3-030-89773-4_6

the prior fifteen years. Kathy is passionate about IDE work, and she was excited to learn that CFC supported ERGs for women and LGBTQ + employees. It's part of what had attracted her to work for CFC.

CFC itself had gone through a huge boom in growth since it was founded in 1990 as a small, family-owned business with one brick-and-mortar store in Columbus, Ohio. Over the past three years, CFC had transitioned from a small business of only 65 people to employing a whopping 1,120 teammates across four locations in the state of Ohio. The majority of the staff worked out of the headquarters in Columbus.

While Kathy loved much of her work at CFC, she had recently become concerned because, during her short time at CFC, a series of concerns had been raised to her by customers and employees. Early in her time at CFC, Kathy began to receive customer complaints about greeting cards. By the time she'd decided to broach the subject, she had received several alarming complaints. Time and again, the issue was the same: a greeting card designed and marketed to coincide with a religious holiday had included incorrect or insensitive language. A different concern was raised regarding e-cards, which had become popular recently. Virtually all of the cards that had been launched had focused on Christian holidays like Easter and Christmas. There were hardly any e-cards honoring other religious holidays, and customers had filed complaints showing they had noticed the omission.

Recently, she had also received a complaint from an employee named Adam who wore a kippah, a traditional Jewish head covering also called a yarmulke, while at work. Adam had experienced a series of perceived microaggressions that worried him. When Adam informed his manager Myrna that he would be taking time off for Yom Kippur, widely considered to be the most important holiday in Jewish religious traditions, Myrna responded by asking, "Are you sure? We really need to meet the project deadline that falls during those dates." Adam continued with his planned leave but felt that he was viewed poorly because of it.

At the same time, Adam had noticed that unlike Myrna's other direct reports, he was not allowed to lead presentations to the executive leadership team. Furthermore, Adam had been passed over for a highly anticipated promotion. Adam was a participant in the company's senior leadership development program and he had been nurtured and prepared for just such an opportunity, so the slight struck him as particularly odd.

He confided in Kathy that he was starting to worry that Myrna felt embarrassed of him and the executive leadership team didn't think he was professional enough due to his kippa and his religious observance. Kathy was deeply concerned by Adam's perceptions, and worried that not only was he disengaging at work but also that he had grounds to file for discrimination if any further issues arose.

Around that time, a group of employees contacted Kathy and HR about establishing a faith-based group for Christian employees at CFC. Kathy was encouraged by this development. Looking at these issues together, it became clear to Kathy that religious diversity already existed at CFC both internally and with their customer base. She felt CFC was not going to be well-served by ignoring religion any longer. She also knew that the topic of religion in the workplace had frequently led to awkward, hostile, and generally uncomfortable conversations. It didn't have to be like that, as Kathy knew from her own time at Mulberry Cards. There was another way: faith-based employee resource groups.

In fact, Kathy and CFC provide a perfect opportunity to explore employee resource groups (ERGs), particularly given the efforts Kathy put forward to research their options. Whereas most of the stories we'll explore in this section are based on research I conducted for my dissertation or are drawn from the news, I've decided to use a more anecdotal story—with all names changed to protect the privacy of those mentioned—because I found it particularly elucidating of the efforts employers can make immediately to create more inclusive environments. As with every other scenario we'll explore in this book, many factors influenced CFC's workplace religious diversity and inclusion efforts, but it was Kathy's keen awareness as an HR professional that helped her identify the potential inclusion of ERGs.

EMPLOYEE RESOURCE GROUPS (ERGs) AND RELIGIOUS DIVERSITY AND INCLUSION

ERGs are employee-led groups that aim to create diverse, inclusive workplaces that harness the power of diverse-thinking to better their organizations and communities. Participation is voluntary and usually based on a shared identity such as gender, race, ethnicity, interest, or religion. ERGs have existed since the 1960s; the first iteration of an ERG emerged at Xerox where Black workers organized to discuss the issues they faced at work.

These groups provide support for employees around career development and personal issues, as well as creating a safe place for employees to discuss the concerns facing them. Many ERGs also welcome participation from allies, people who do not share the same identity but who care for the groups' rights.

According to Forbes (Huang, 2017), ERGs can be found in 90% of *Fortune 500* companies and lead to benefits like:

- Improving working conditions physically and emotionally.
- Bringing employees together for exchange and understanding.
- Nurturing leadership qualities in minority groups.
- Addressing company-wide issues.
- Bringing to the surface buried tensions that need to be addressed.

As with other ERGs based on a shared identity, some organizations have faith-based ERGs. Though they are not nearly as common as groups based on other identities, faith-based ERGs have been on the rise in recent years (Crary, 2020). In fact, more than 20% of the *Fortune* 100 currently have faith-based ERGs established.

Faith-based ERGs can be comprised of people from one religion or faith or multiple religions or faiths. They often meet to discuss the relation of one's religious identity to company culture, holidays, and accommodations. Some religion-specific ERGs also provide a safe place for on-site prayer and worship, fasting, mentorship, and service projects. Akin to other ERGs, there are numerous benefits that faith-based ERGs bring to the workplace, including:

- A reduction in religious bias and discrimination.
- Improved morale and employee retention.
- Sensitivity to potential issues before they arise, enabling an organization to be proactive rather than responsive.
- Decreased misunderstandings between employees from different religious groups.
- Insight into products and services designed with religious users in mind.

In an increasingly diverse world, it's clear that faith-based ERGs can provide a means for inclusion and belonging for religiously diverse people while also shoring up an organization's processes to ensure public-facing initiatives are well thought out.

There are three models of faith-based ERGs: the religion-specific ERG, the interfaith ERG, and the interfaith network (Tanenbaum, 2014). A religion-specific ERG convenes members of a single religion to support one another. An interfaith ERG gathers members from any or no religious background for interfaith dialogue and support. Finally, the interfaith network ERG comes into play mostly in very large organizations that have many individual religion-specific ERGs, and functions as an umbrella organization to oversee the work of the individual ERGs (Tanenbaum, 2014). Like with other ERGs, allies of any faith or those who are agnostic or atheistic are welcomed at these employee-hosted meetings.

Existence of one religion-specific ERG doesn't mean that every religion represented at an organization must have an ERG, nor is it practical or feasible for every single religion to have its own ERG. As with other kinds of ERGs, faith-based ERGs must submit a proposed group charter; state the ERG's purpose and mission; identify an executive sponsor, leadership team, and potential members; and make a case to the organization about why it should support the establishment of the group. In short, the group's business case must be in alignment with the diversity and inclusion strategy and core values and beliefs of the organization (Tanenbaum, 2014). In this vein, it is important for organizations to make all requirements for ERGs clear, including making sure all employees know that they cannot form an ERG for the purpose of opposing another group or promoting political positions. While ERGs do require the support of an organization, the organization does not establish ERGs for employees—employees establish ERGs for themselves.

To understand the two most common forms of faith-based ERGs, let's look at some real-world examples from American Express and Salesforce.

Many organizations have single-faith ERGs, including Target, Apple, Ameriprise, and American Express. American Express, a publicly traded, multinational financial services corporation that was founded in 1850, has sixteen ERGs, which they call employee networks, that have helped them not only with product development but also to plan cultural events for current employees and potential applicants (American Express, 2021; Faith Driven Investor, 2022; Tanenbaum, 2014). Their three religion-specific employee networks even helped them create gift cards to celebrate Diwali and Chanukah (Tanenbaum, 2014). The three religion-specific ERGs are:

1. CHAI—a Jewish employee network that draws its name from the Hebrew word for life. The network hosts educational and community events to raise awareness of Jewish culture and it serves as a resource for members.
2. PEACE—a Muslim employee network that draws its name from one of the meanings of the word Islam. PEACE focuses on creating awareness, understanding, and education to counter the misinformation surrounding Muslims and Islam.
3. SALT—a Christian employee network that draws its name from the many references to salt as a symbol of permanence, loyalty, and fidelity in the Bible. This group is dedicated to providing resources to Christian employees of American Express and demonstrating a commitment to the values of the company.

Together and independently, these groups host educational and community events such as lunch and learns and informational booths in an effort to bring awareness of their religions and counter stereotypes. The groups act as resource and support networks for their members. American Express also leans on these groups to provide advice based on their expertise when planning ethnic and cultural events, organizing recruiting initiatives to attract diverse talent, and strategizing on how to market to multicultural communities (American Express, 2017, 2021; Tanenbaum, 2014).

Interfaith or multi-faith ERGs, which bring together employees of diverse religious or faith traditions, also exist at several high-profile organizations including Google, Meta (formerly Facebook), and Salesforce. Founded in 1999, Salesforce is a publicly traded, cloud-based software company that creates and supports customer relationship management software. Salesforce has 35,000 employees, and it currently supports twelve ERGs called equality groups. Nearly half of all employees participate in at least one equality group; to honor the significant efforts made by those in these groups, Salesforce offers recognition and compensation for globally elected Equality Group leaders (Salesforce, 2021).

Salesforce's interfaith group, Faithforce, is one of the fastest growing faith-based ERGs. It launched in 2017 to celebrate, support, and foster understanding of faith and spirituality through inclusive events and initiatives, including educational events and initiatives. All are welcome in the group, even those who do not affiliate with any religion or do not consider themselves to be spiritual (Warnke, 2019). Muslims, Christians, Jews, Sikhs, Hindus, pagans, and humanists are all represented in the group. Since its founding, Faithforce has attracted more than 2,600 employees (Crary, 2020).

Notably, Faithforce has leveraged its platform to address religious tragedies. For example, when the Tree of Life Synagogue was attacked in Pittsburgh in October 2018, the group came together to organize a religious vigil across seven locations worldwide. This vigil was led by Rabbi Michael Lesak of Glide Memorial. Jewish employees were able to express their pain, while their colleagues were given a chance to show their support. Employees, along with a Salesforce match, donated thousands of dollars to the Anti-Defamation League (ADL) (Warnke, 2019).

These examples not only provide interesting insight into the practical implementation of faith-based ERGs, but also illuminate an important concept for the religiously diverse workplace: bridging and bonding social capital.

Religion-specific ERGs are in alignment with the concept of bonding social capital, whereas interfaith ERGs connect more with the concept of bridging social capital. Bonding happens within a group or community, whereas bridging occurs across diverse groups. When we apply this concept to the religion-specific model, members of each group will be bonding and innovating with those who belong to their group while also bridging with those in the other religion-specific groups. The interfaith ERG model focuses more on the bridging of people of various religions within the one group. It can be argued that bonding can lead to stronger and more meaningful relationships than bridging (Claridge, 2018; Park et al., 2014).

PRACTICAL CONSIDERATIONS FOR FAITH-BASED ERGs

Given the many variables at play in the decision to form faith-based ERGs, it is understandable that many feel intimidated and unsure where to start. That said, there are some factors to weigh-in if your organization is considering forming faith-based ERGs, including:

- Existing ERGs—Any new ERGs, and faith-based ERGs are no exception, should be in line with existing ERGs in terms of how they're founded and what their charter should include. This is true whether the faith-based ERG is planned to be interfaith or religion-specific.

- Company size—Company size is important because although no one size fits all when it comes to which type of faith-based ERG should be implemented, organizations of less than 1,000 employees are better off implementing a religion-specific ERG model than an interfaith ERG model because their workforce typically lacks the religious diversity needed to support an interfaith ERG model (Tanenbaum, 2014).
- Diversity of leadership—The composition of your leadership team and other mid-level leaders is important when considering forming an ERG. If leaders are all from one religious group, then there will naturally be some favoritism shown to that religion, whether intentional or not. Favoritism can lead to in-fighting and ultimately become counterproductive when it comes to an interfaith ERG. If, however, your leadership is very religiously diverse, an interfaith ERG may help foster leadership in your workforce.
- Bonding and bridging—It is important to know when to accept an ERG's charter and when to deny it. If your organization wants to open up dialogue between religious groups and create understanding, the interfaith model will be more focused on helping people bond across identities. If you have a faith group that is uniquely struggling, the religion-specific model will help the members of that group bond and troubleshoot together inside of their group, while bridging with other faith-specific ERGs.

If your organization doesn't have faith-based ERGs, start by assessing the above factors and deciding if it's something your employees would benefit from and have the energy to create and sustain.

If employees decide to have a singular religion-specific ERG, implementation will likely bring with it additional special considerations. For instance, it is imperative that the company be prepared to answer questions from their employees as to why one religion-specific ERG may be permitted while another one is not. The qualifications and requirements to establish a religion-specific ERG must be fairly applied to all groups. ERGs in general need to make a business case as to why the company should support their establishment, which must be in alignment with the organization's overall diversity and inclusion strategy (Tanenbaum, 2014).

Many of these considerations are the exact ones Kathy faced as she reviewed the models for faith-based ERGs. When she approached her CEO to discuss supporting the creation of a faith-based ERG, she felt certain the right path forward would be in supporting the founding of religion-specific ERGs. Her CEO, who had been with the company since it was founded in 1990, brought different ideas to the table. While he was initially resistant to any kind of faith-based ERG out of fear of costly litigation, negative publicity, and potential backlash from employees, he came around to the idea of an interfaith ERG, rather than a faith-specific one, particularly when he considered the inspiring work of Faithforce.

While there truly is no single way to decide which faith-based ERGs are right for each organization, CFC came to a conclusion based on the factors we identified above:

- Existing ERGs—They considered their existing ERGs and how they were chartered, identifying that a faith-based ERG could add a lot to the experiences of employees and should easily be in alignment with the company's IDE mission.
- Company size—CFC employs 1,120 people across four locations, all within the state of Ohio. The religion-specific model is typically recommended for companies with fewer than 1,000 employees because they may lack religiously diverse leaders, which is a requirement when implementing an interfaith-religious ERG or interfaith network (Tanenbaum, 2014). The interfaith ERG is also preferable because CFC has multiple locations and overseeing the initiatives of religion-specific ERGs across multiple locations can become burdensome and overwhelming (Tanenbaum, 2014).
- Diversity of leadership—Kathy knew that there were leaders of many religious backgrounds at the CFC, including the CEO she spoke with who is Christian and attends church weekly. Furthermore, the Director of Accounting was Jewish—something the concerned employee, Adam, never learned and thus could not see that the organization was invested in leaders who are Jewish. Religious diversity in senior leadership is an important element of making faith-based ERGs work well.
- Other considerations—Finally, given the CEO's concerns about litigation as a result of faith-based ERGs, an interfaith ERG is a great path forward. Conflict over inclusion as an official ERG may arise more frequently with religion-specific models, because if the

company sponsors a group for one religion and not another, regardless of whether the reasoning is valid, employees will automatically question whether they are being wrongly denied organizing. The interfaith network is not recommended in this case as it is considered to be an overarching organization that supports multiple individual religion-specific ERGs (Tanenbaum, 2014).

A lot of thought must go into forming ERGs as the nuance and context of your organization will greatly change how these factors are viewed, and they will influence your ultimate decision.

Assessing the Level of Religious Inclusion at CFC

As an organization, CFC is at Level 1: Avoidance, but is attempting to reach Level 2: Compliance, in part through the institution of faith-based ERGs. Religious diversity and inclusion are still relatively new concepts to the organization, brought to leadership's attention by Kathy. While Kathy has a deep passion for IDE efforts, and she probably likely wants religiously diverse employees to feel included, she acted in part due to fear of legal exposure if CFC didn't start acting. To truly reach Compliance, CFC will need to complete a compliance audit and training to help them identify where they are and are not compliant with the law. They haven't done so before, a potentially costly oversight the CFC leadership should address immediately.

CFC demonstrates that there are many ways organizations intersect with religion already: with customers, employees, and even products and services. Each opens an organization up to potentially costly issues whether legal or regarding reputation. When an organization decides to make religious diversity and inclusion part of their mission by ensuring they're compliant with laws or encouraging employees to form ERGs they have the opportunity to not only provide workers with better work environments but also to tap into the knowledge and resources of religiously diverse employees to improve their products and services and better serve their customers.

Faith-based ERGs are just one possible religious IDE initiative an organization can engage in. There are many others from recruitment efforts to how you measure your diversity efforts that are also integral to a holistic and inclusive approach to religious diversity and inclusion. In the next chapter, we'll explore how one public service organization grappled with these issues over decades.

REFERENCES

American Express. (2017). *Employee networks at American Express.* https://www.americanexpress.com/content/dam/amex/us/staticassets/pdf/global-diversity-and-inclusion/American_Express_Employee_Networks_June_2017.pdf

American Express. (2021). *Careers: Inclusion and diversity at American Express: Our commitment.* https://www.americanexpress.com/en-us/careers/inclusion-and-diversity/index.html/?intlink=us-amex-career-en-us-home-details-learnmore

Claridge, T. (2018). What is the difference between bonding and bridging social capital? *Social Capital Research.* https://www.socialcapitalresearch.com/difference-bonding-bridging-social-capital/

Crary, D. (2020, February 11). More US firms are boosting faith-based support for employees. *AP News.* https://apnews.com/article/financial-markets-us-news-business-ap-top-news-religion-d81dae462a668ee08a5fd58f1c410173

Faith Driven Investor. (2022). *Companies with Faith Based employee resource groups.* https://www.faithdriveninvestor.org/information-on-companies-with-ergs

Huang, G. (2017, November 13). 90% of Fortune 500 companies already have a solution to gender equality but aren't utilizing it. *Forbes.* https://www.forbes.com/sites/georgenehuang/2017/11/13/90-of-fortune-500-companies-already-have-a-solution-to-gender-equality-but-arent-utilizing-it/?sh=6f53194c1c34

Park, J. Z., Griebel Rogers, J., Neubert, M. J., & Dougherty, K. D. (2014). Workplace-bridging religious capital: Connecting congregations to work outcomes. *Sociology of Religion, 75*(2), 309–331. https://doi.org/10.1093/socrel/sru012

Salesforce. (2021). *We believe in equity for all.* https://www.salesforce.com/company/equality/#eq-sf-ohana

Tanenbaum Center for Interreligious Understanding. (2014). *Faith-based employee resource groups: a Tanenbaum report for corporate members.* https://tanenbaum.org/wp-content/uploads/2014/08/Tanenbaums-2014-Report-for-Corporate-Members.pdf

Warnke, S. (2019, August 22). Faithforce: A place of healing. *LinkedIn.* https://www.linkedin.com/pulse/faithforce-place-healing-sue-warnke/

Including Sikhs, Muslims, and Rastafarians in the London Metropolitan Police Force

Abstract Inclusion, diversity, and equity (IDE) in public service organizations have become a political priority across the Western world. Nowhere, perhaps, has the challenge of advancing IDE been more problematic than in the police force, where the relationship between the police and ethnic, racial, and religious minorities is often fraught. This chapter's case study of the London Metropolitan Police Force includes an in-depth analysis of the evolution of their religious and cultural diversity initiatives over the last three decades or so. The case clearly illustrates that despite uneven or slow progress, IDE goals are achievable.

Keywords Sikhs · Muslims and Rastafarians · Religious garb and grooming · Kaizen HC model of religious inclusion · Police and minorities · London Metropolitan Police

In 2011, Chief Superintendent Dal Babu decided to retire from his job at the London Metropolitan Police Force (the Met) after being passed over for promotion. Babu's promotion was denied supposedly due to his limited skills in dealing with the media, despite the fact that he has a master's degree, speaks four languages, is a recipient of the Order of the British Empire award, and once served as a spokesperson for

© The Author(s), under exclusive license to Springer Nature   89
Switzerland AG 2022
E. Hasan, *Embracing Workplace Religious Diversity and Inclusion*,
Palgrave Studies in Equity, Diversity, Inclusion, and Indigenization
in Business, https://doi.org/10.1007/978-3-030-89773-4_7

Muslim police officers on TV. Furthermore, the London borough of Harrow, which he oversaw, experienced markedly increased confidence in the police during his tenure (Laville, 2013).

Babu had fought long and hard to keep doing his job, having won a landmark case against the Met several years earlier after demonstrating that he had failed to receive a promotion and experienced discrimination because he is Muslim. At the time of his retirement, he reflected on how the Met had changed, noting that racist name-calling had become less common, but that there had been no significant gain in Black and ethnic minority officers over thirty years. He told *The Guardian* (Laville, 2013), "We have not managed to replicate the communities we serve. Our major cities are majority ethnic minority and yet the police force remains stubbornly white. We have ended up with lots of theory around police and diversity, and what we need is an ounce of action."

As the most senior Muslim Asian Chief Superintendent, Babu's resignation sent ripples through the Met, London, and even the UK as a whole. He had served as a mentor to many up-and-coming Black and ethnic minority officers, many of whom moved up the ranks.

Furthermore, many of his named complaints—that there were few opportunities for advancement for Black and ethnic minority officers, that recruitment efforts should focus on diverse groups, and that officers should be recruited from the communities they serve—became initiatives that would radically change the face of the Met over the coming years. Public service organizations, including law enforcement, rely on public cooperation and acceptance to complete their work. In such environments, religious inclusivity can become chaotic and complicated given the wide array of religions and beliefs (or lack thereof) that people bring with them to a given situation. But where do public service organizations draw the line on inclusivity while making possible reasonable accommodations for religious expression and practice? Do inclusive regulations in regard to religious dress and appearance go far enough? If they conflict with their religious beliefs, should officers be able to disregard director orders or refuse assignments? (Grunloh, 2005).

Over the last two decades, in many countries, institutions like the police have had to adapt and make room for the ambiguities and complexities of the religious beliefs of employees and the communities they serve. After being faced with many high-profile instances of religious discrimination, the Met has become a leader around religiously inclusive policing within the UK and Europe.

Public service organizations can adapt to and make room for the ambiguities and complexities of accommodating and including diverse employees with different religious beliefs. It's a matter of making it a priority and being responsive to the communities you serve.

RELIGION IN THE UK

Harkening back to the sixteenth century up through today, Christianity, first under the guise of Roman Catholicism and then the Church of England, has been the dominant religion in the UK. Judaism was made illegal in 1290 in the UK—despite this fact, Judaism rose again in the nineteenth century and grew alongside other religions as immigrants streamed into urban communities. Many Jewish people came from Eastern Europe and the U.S., while a large proportion of Muslims came from the Arab world and parts of South Asia and sub-Saharan Africa, particularly Pakistan, Bangladesh, Somalia, Sudan, and Ethiopia. Concurrently, other religious communities like the Hindus, Sikhs, and Buddhist originated from India and China.

While a significant amount of migration occurred from countries the UK colonized, the highest influx of migrants dates back to after the Second World War following huge labor shortages and demands in declining industrial cities in the UK (Abass, 2017). Contrary to the prediction of scholars of religion that immigrants from colonized countries would assimilate and quickly adapt to the norms and values of British society and national culture (Gay, 1971), the opposite occurred. The influx of migrants and settlers changed the religious landscape of the country, especially the city of London where most newcomers tended to settle for economic reasons. Migrants who settled in Britain brought with them their cultures and beliefs, conversely forcing, albeit slowly, acceptance and inclusion in their new environment.

Today, religion in the UK takes on new forms, and while some religions are steadily growing, others are waning (ONS, 2019). Here are the trends that have arisen in recent years:

- The percentage of the UK population that identifies as Christian dropped from 71.8 to 50.4% between 2001 and 2018.

- People self-reporting to be Muslims and Hindus have each risen steadily. Between 2001 and 2018, the percentage of the population that identifies as Muslim rose from 3.0 to 5.8% while those identifying as Hindus grew from 1.1 to 1.7%.
- The percentage of the population identifying as Jewish, Buddhist, and Sikh held relatively steady at 0.6, 0.4, and 0.7%, respectively.
- Notably, 38.8% of the population reported having no religious affiliation in 2018, up from 14.8% in 2001.
- The most diverse region was London with the largest number of people identifying as Muslim, Buddhist, Hindu, and Jewish residing there.

Today, there are a number of mosques, gurdwaras, and mandirs all over the UK, and it is estimated that less than half of the population in the UK identify as Christians. Pew Research Center predicts this trajectory will continue: In 2050, Christians will make up 45.4% of the population, Muslims 11.3%, Hindus 2.0%, Buddhists 0.9%, Jews and folk religions each 0.3%, and no religious affiliation will reach 38.9%.

Keeping these statistics in mind, Steven Vertovec, interestingly, coined the term superdiversity to describe the UK. Superdiversity recognizes both the high level of diversity found between minority groups *and* within them (2007). Citizens as well as refugees, asylum seekers, and undocumented immigrants can belong to the same ethnic group. But while they share some common identity, they still have diverse experiences and needs. In this vein, the complex interplay of various diversity factors has combined to make the UK one of the most diverse countries in the world ethnically, racially, and religiously—and London is a bustling metropolitan filled with people with diverse religious affiliations, making it a challenging climate for work.

The Met's Long and Challenging History with Diversity

In 1829, the Metropolitan Police Service was founded as the first modern police force in England. The force began with about 1,000 white, male officers policing a population of less than two million. White women were prohibited from joining the force until the First World War when a voluntary organization called Women's Police Service began to assist the police in unofficial capacities.

As the policing needs of the city evolved and the population grew, more officers were hired, leading to the hiring of white women in 1919. Though working full-time and placed in the same ranks with their male colleagues, female officers had limited responsibilities, and could not remain in the force if they married. These policies continued until the end of the Second World War when crime rates rose drastically, and in order to accommodate more officers, the rules had to change.

By 1974, the service had fully integrated Black and ethnic minority women and men, offering financial parity; officers at the same level were given equal pay regardless of their ethnicity. Not surprisingly, very low numbers of ethnic minorities showed an interest in joining the service due to the prevalent systemic racism they experienced.

By the late 1990s, Black minority groups had made a series of calls for more racial diversity; there were also accusations of racism against minority officers within the Met (Haves, 2020). White officers reported increasing resistance from ethnic minority communities; furthermore, there weren't enough officers from such communities within the force despite the reality that the population of London had become increasingly diverse.

In 2000, the Home Office, the department that regulates police forces in the UK, introduced a new strategy of setting recruitment targets for ethnic minorities in order to create a balance in officer numbers within communities. The Met had been given a target to reach 26% of ethnic minority police officers by 2009, but by 2003, only 9.8% of the officers in the Met were from minority backgrounds (BBC, 2014). The target could not be achieved for several reasons including the reputation of the force as a racist, sexist, and xenophobic organization, making attracting the targeted groups difficult and the low retention rate for minority officers. Many left during probation or after two years, so there were very few role models in high ranks to attract younger officers (Bhugowandeen, 2013).

Following 9/11, Muslim and Sikh officers all over Britain experienced increased hostilities from the public as well as from some of their colleagues who suddenly treated them differently even though they had been in the force for years. Among the semi-senior ranks, officers from ethnic minority groups claimed that they experienced discrimination in promotion due to their ethnicity and even their faith. In 2008, a female Muslim senior civilian manager named Yasmin Rehman raised a claim of racial and sexual discrimination at the Employment Tribunal. Ironically, she was at the time in charge of promoting racial and religious diversity within the Met. She later withdrew the case after settlement but had to step down from her role (Greenwood, 2009). It is during this time that Chief Superintendent Dal Babu resigned from his position at the Met.

These events and more did nothing to attract a diverse workforce, so although London's population diversity kept increasing, the Met's frontline remained significantly less diverse than the communities it served.

Introducing Diversity and Inclusion Initiatives

In a bid to restore its tainted reputation, the Met instituted a new plan in 2001 titled "Protect and Respect: Everybody Benefits." The program was designed to send a clear message that the Met was truly committed to inclusivity within the service. As you can see from the instances of discrimination we've explored in this chapter dating to as recently as 2013, the program didn't immediately translate to the Met becoming more inclusive. However, for the first time, religious diversity took a central role in this strategy and over time, there have been incredible results.

The Home Office engaged in several initiatives including recognizing festival and holy days in different religions to enable officers from varying faith groups to participate in religious observance. Furthermore, prayer rooms and creches were created at big stations, and Scotland Yard's canteen began to serve Halal food.

Religious turbans and headscarves in the Met's colors were also incorporated into police uniforms. Finally, Muslim female officers were officially allowed to wear four different types of hijabs when on duty, a significant move toward including more women from ethnic minorities in the Met's workforce. This move was a follow-up to the approved policy for Sikh officers who were permitted to wear turbans with their uniforms while on duty (Hopkins, 2001). During the same period, leadership at the Met considered adjustments that could be made to allow Rastafarians who wanted to join the police to keep their locks (Sal, 2000). While there were safety concerns around the Rastafarian hairstyle given its length, it was agreed that there could be safe ways to incorporate locks into the uniform to include this important group of people in the Met.

The new focus on religious diversity and making practical changes to become more accommodating of religiously diverse people had a significant impact on other police units around the region. The Thames Valley police, then in charge of an area outside London, recognized the Met's successes and set up Operation Comfort that sent officers from minority ethnicities with high cultural awareness and language skills to connect with locals for positive impact building. Officers were sent into mosques and other community and religious gatherings to relate one on one with people and, for the first time, ethnic minority officers were welcomed to be themselves and utilize their diverse hidden talents without the overpowering need to conform once in their uniforms. Shortly after, the strategy became popular among other police units in Britain, and the opportunities presented by diversity and diverse talents became more visible.

Clearly things were changing, and it was almost certain that diversity and inclusion could provide the potential for improvements in service delivery to communities and wider development across the service.

RELIGIOUS INCLUSION THROUGH TARGETED RECRUITMENT

The Home Office has legitimized religious inclusion through supporting organizations like Inter Faith Group to advance public understanding of different religious groups and through setting targeted goals for police units around the UK (Weller et al., 2001). Legislation preventing such targeted recruitment was overridden in some cases, especially in the case of police units that struggled to reach targets due to low percentages of minorities in their communities of operation. One very popular example was the Police Service Northern Ireland who implemented a 50:50 recruitment policy to make the service representative of the predominant religions in their communities: Catholicism and Protestant Christianity (*The Irish Times*, 2010).

At the Met, other measures were introduced including a fast-track program to recruit twenty experienced officers from the public and private sectors directly to the rank of superintendents, as well as a plan to attract university graduates. Both programs, introduced in 2014, attempted to increase the diversity of the Met by attracting people with diverse backgrounds and perspectives. While Boris Johnson was Mayor of London in 2014 he announced the introduction of a residence-based approach for recruitment to the Met. This approach required potential applicants to have resided in London for at least three of the previous six years in order to be eligible to join the force at entry level. Following the policy, the number of ethnic minority recruits to the force doubled in just one year (Mayor of London, 2015). This residency requirement was reintroduced in 2020 to help the Met successfully achieve a target of 40% ethnic minority representation.

In April 2021, the UK Commission on Race and Ethnic Disparities informed the Home Office that officers needed to be equipped with local know-how, especially an understanding of different languages, religions, and cultural sensitivities in their communities of operation. It was clear that increasing representation through legislation had not been sufficient to drive the required changes. The focus needed to shift to implementing programs rooted in fairness, equity, and respect for all groups of people (Brown, 2021).

There are two main ways this focus manifested: in the Met's diversity and inclusion strategy and with employee support networks.

The Met's Diversity and Inclusion Strategy

The Met's strategy for inclusion, diversity, and engagement, called STRIDE, acknowledges the existence of racism, discrimination, and bias within the force, especially the lack of diverse candidates in the pipeline for senior positions. The number of new Black and ethnic minority recruits jumped from 16% in 2014–2015 to 28% in 2015–2016, holding steady through 2017. The Met even won Personnel Today's Award for Diversity and Inclusion in 2017 (McCulloch, 2017).

In April 2021, STRIDE was re-engineered to drive the Met's operations up through 2025, outlining how the organization would purposefully institute strategic change in its approach to policing, community engagement, internal management, and representation within the force. STRIDE is broken down into four programs: Protection, Engagement, Equality, and Learning.

Most relevant for our purposes is the program on Equality, which focuses on building and growing a diverse and inclusive organization that is representative of the city of London, where employees from diverse groups can belong wholly without bias, discrimination, bullying, and other negative treatment. According to the leadership at the Met, STRIDE maps out an action plan aimed at attracting new recruits from ethnic minority backgrounds through recruitment outreach programs, apprenticeship programs, and buddy programs for part-time recruits from ethnic minority groups (Metropolitan Police, 2021). It also maps out a career development service that will focus on prioritizing the advancement of women and employees from other underrepresented groups by providing workshops and other learning resources to support these officers through their development within the force.

The results of this program will be monitored and measured internally and periodically by the STRIDE board, and externally every three months by an oversight board as part of the Met's performance framework (Metropolitan Police, 2021).

Employee Support Networks

The Met encourages the formation of and provides developmental support to religion-based ERGs, which it calls Religious Employee Associations. These associations support the recruitment, advancement, and retention of affiliated officers and provide opportunities for networking between members (Metropolitan Police, 2021). Some of the popular networks include the Jewish Police Association, the Metropolitan Police Hindu Association, the Muslim Police Association, the Metropolitan Police Humanists, and the Metropolitan Police Sikh Association.

These groups face outward, sometimes sending members to recruit new hires at major religious and community events, and inward. Internally, for example, the Muslim Police Association advocated for the introduction of hijabs for female officers, halal food and facilities for Salaah (prayers), and permission for traditional dress to be allowed when not on duty. The British Sikh Police Association advocated for the introduction of ballistic turbans to enable Sikh service men to serve as firearms officers; according to the Association of Chief Police Officers, although implementation may be light years ahead, future exploration isn't altogether ruled out (*The Telegraph*, 2010).

While these associations have made critical strides toward promoting the interests of their members, there is still much the Met could do to be inclusive of and create belonging for religious people, especially in cases where their activities or dress are sacred and do not disrupt their work.

THE MET'S ROLE IN THE FUTURE
OF RELIGIOUS DIVERSITY AT WORK

In some ways, examining how the police have become more inclusive may feel counterintuitive to our wider discussion of religious inclusion and freedom. But the truth is that the Met is an incredible example of a public institution grappling with religious inclusion in the workforce and in the wider community. Why aren't there similar examples from social service or health care? There very well may be, but the recent focus on police accountability over the last few decades means these issues and initiatives are high-profile and well-documented. Regardless of our personal opinions of the police and policing, the relevance of the case is undeniable.

London provides a picture of what a society looks like when it becomes religiously and ethnically diverse—it's a hint of what lies ahead in large cities. Public service work is inherently complex, and the Met demonstrates clearly that public service organizations can and should adapt to and make room for the complexities of inclusion and belonging for religiously diverse employees. When we do so, we also allow employees to use their unique identities to effectively provide valued service within the communities that they serve.

Today, the Met is the largest police force in the UK with about 43,000 officers and staff policing most of London and serving at the heart of national culture (Brown, 2021). Even though the country is largely secular, leadership at the Met recognizes, accommodates, and even celebrates religious differences among employees. The culture is changing from merely paying lip service to taking practical measures to ensure every employee's voice is heard, regardless of their creed.

However, to ensure continuity of effective policing in such a large and culturally diverse city as London, the Met will need to keep evolving in its strategies toward maintaining religious inclusion. A long road lies ahead, and the Met must create real inclusivity for religiously diverse employees.

Lessons Organizations Can Draw from the Met

While many remain critical of the Met's IDE efforts, there is much we can learn from the Met's long journey around religious diversity and inclusion as we create more inclusive workplaces, particularly given how the Met provides a peek into the diverse societies and workplaces of the future.

You may be tempted to think you have plenty of time before you'll face the breadth and depth of the diversity of the Met, but it's likely to occur sooner than you think. And, just with everything else in running an organization, you want to see the trends coming and develop a plan so you can be responsive to changing times. (In Chapter 10, we'll talk more about what the future holds for workplace religious diversity and inclusion).

To develop a robust, responsive, and effective IDE strategy, you can take the following five steps:

1. *Assess the current state of your organization through data collection.*— The first step is to figure out where you are as an organization right now. This means listening to your employees, clients, customers, and colleagues about their religious identities and needs. It may sound obvious, but many established organizations propel forward giving little thought to how their employees, clients, customers, and colleagues are changing or how their needs aren't being met. The Met, of course, is a huge organization with many different means of accountability from governmental regulations to social movements dedicated to reform. Your organization may not face those same pressures, but that doesn't mean you shouldn't be asking yourself how you can be more inclusive of religiously diverse people. And, if you don't have the same spotlight on you that means you can be proactive in your data collection from constituents to make sure your organization is as responsive and inclusive as it can be. Gathering feedback can look like many things from conducting an anonymous survey to informal conversations with employees about how their religious identity is or isn't included in the organization to a formal focus groups conducted by a third party.

2. *Decide where you want to be.*—Now that you have a sense of where you are, think about where you want to be in terms of religious inclusion. In other words, this is when you begin to develop a robust religious IDE strategy. You need to be able to measure your success and to ensure you're headed in the direction you want, you're going to have to dig into the numbers. You don't want to be where the Met was when Chief Superintendent Babu retired: having made some cultural changes, but not making any significant increase in the actual number of new diverse employees hired. Creating a religious IDE strategy will require time and effort because you will need to research demographics of your society and community and the

current makeup of your organization and pair that with the feedback you gathered as part of Step 1, as well as current research on
managing religious diversity and inclusion. Then, you'll need to see
how your religious IDE strategy feeds into your greater IDE strategy
and how you'll help leaders at all levels of your organization increase
their focus on religious inclusion. Finally, you'll want to make sure
you give all of your constituents an opportunity to review, react to,
and help develop a new version of your IDE strategy so it reaches
the people it's designed to *and* leads to the outcomes you desire.

3. *Analyze the gap between your current and desired state.*—You know
where you are and you know where you need to be. Now's the
time to identify what steps you can take to close the gaps you see
in your religious inclusion. For instance, this might be when you
engage in targeted recruitment to diversify your organization. Many
are tempted to jump right to recruitment efforts when it comes to
matters of diversity and inclusion. As we discussed in Chapter 2,
that impulse emphasizes diversity but doesn't follow through with
inclusion. That's why I recommend making this a later step in
your efforts. So often organizations start with recruitment, successfully recruit amazing new people to their team, and then cannot
retain them as employees because the organizational culture wasn't
ready to be truly inclusive of diverse religious people. Oftentimes
in these cases, new hires are made so thoroughly to feel as if they
don't belong that they move on quickly. So while addressing gaps is
important, it shouldn't be your first step.

4. *Implement a few evidence-based religious IDE initiatives directly in
response to the concerns and feedback of your constituents.*—Once
you've completed information gathering and planning, it's important to show that you're taking action. Identify an initiative or two
that are attainable and small in scale to test out more inclusive
policies. For instance, the Met had many initiatives it implemented
in response to employee concerns, including developing prayer
rooms for employee-use, evaluating their uniforms and dress code
to include religious dress for Sikhs, Muslims, and Rastafarians, and
creating flexibility for employees to identify and observe their own
holy days, rather than those designated by the government.

5. *Evaluate the success of your initiatives through data collection.*—The
quick version of this step is: Once you've done steps 1 through 4
once, do them again. And then do them again. Then do that forever.

The truth is that the only way we can have truly responsive IDE strategies that include religious identity at the top of the agenda is to revisit them frequently. This results in an iterative process that leads to the best possible strategy to respond to that moment in time and the people actually present at your organization. Specifically, this entails having a means of data collection so you can assess the success of each initiative. Not only is this important to help you make the argument for more inclusion to your leaders or board, but it also helps make sure some objectivity is brought to the process. The last thing you would want is for the success of an initiative to come down to whether or not a single person felt it was worth it. So if your organization implemented holy day flexibility—allowing employees to self-select when they would be out and for which observances— you might use a survey to measure how many people took advantage of this policy, to what degree it made them feel more included, how they feel it impacted their productivity (positively, negatively, or not at all), and the like.

I use a version of this gap analysis model in my consulting work as a part of our organizational development and change model. It's a fairly straightforward process that requires a significant commitment of time and energy from leadership and the organization as a whole. That said, you have the opportunity to take proactive steps today to develop the kind of IDE strategy that can transform your organization and create real inclusion and belonging for religiously diverse employees. As we saw with the Met, this process can take many decades and missteps—and many people were discouraged, injured, and dehumanized along the way. Don't wait until something goes wrong to have a religious IDE strategy.

Assessing the Level of Religious Inclusion at the Met

At the time of writing, the Met hovers between being a Level 2: Compliance organization and a Level 3: Emerging organization. Historically, however, some could argue that the Met has been at each level of the Kaizen HC Model of Religious Inclusion at one time or another. In many ways, the Met been a model for how public service organizations and all employers can make space for religious diversity at the workplace. From their ERGs to allowing religious attire and even incorporating it into their uniforms to setting aggressive, public IDE ethnic and religious diversity goals, they've made a substantive commitment to diversity and inclusion around gender, race, ethnicity, and religion. At the same time, reports of rampant abusive and discriminatory language and behaviors among Met officers continue to emerge (Kotecha, 2022).

As they become an Emerging organization, the Met can continue to focus on the recruitment and, particularly, the retention of Black and ethnic minorities. More proactive engagement with their faith-based ERGs could also help the Met be more responsive to concerns that might be buried just below the surface. They can also develop a more focused strategy for religious inclusion, not solely relying on ethnic diversity to help with religious diversity. Finally, the Met can take an external stance advocating for ethnic and religious inclusion in the UK and beyond, particularly in addressing Islamophobia.

The Met's trajectory as a religiously inclusive organization provides promising evidence that concerted effort can yield compelling results—even a long-standing, large organization with a history of discrimination can do better by instituting policies and initiatives that honor and value religious diversity. By implementing a carefully thought out and measured IDE strategy that spans the continuum of employment from recruitment through retention, the Met has defined a path for success for itself as an organization in a diverse cultural environment. In the next chapter, we'll explore how the intersection of culture and religion can influence a workplace and the treatment of employees.

References

Abass, T. (2017). After 9/11: British South Asian Muslims, Islamophobia, multiculturalism, and the State. *The American Journal of Islamic Social Sciences, 21*, 3.

BBC. (2014, March 27). *Met police chief backs 50:50 recruitment.* https://www.bbc.com/news/uk-england-london-26765540

Bhugowandeen, B. (2013). *Diversity in the British police: Adapting to a multicultural society.* https://doi.org/10.4000/mimmoc.1340

Brown, J. (2021, September 29). *Policing in the UK. Research briefing. House of Commons Library.* https://commonslibrary.parliament.uk/research-briefings/cbp-8582/

Gay, J. D. (1971). *The geography of religion in England.* Duck-worth.

Greenwood, C. (2009, January 14). Police equality chief drops discrimination claim. *The Independent.* https://www.independent.co.uk/news/uk/crime/police-equality-chief-drops-discrimination-claim-1366044.html

Grunloh, K. A. (2005) Religious accommodations for police officers: A comparative analysis of religious accommodation law in the United States, Canada, and The United Kingdom. Political Science. *Indiana International and Comparative Law Review, 16*(1). https://doi.org/10.18060/17857

Haves, E. (2020). Accusations of racism in the Metropolitan Police Service. *House of Lords Library.* https://lordslibrary.parliament.uk/accusations-of-racism-in-the-metropolitan-police-service/

Hopkins, N. (2001, April 24). Met lets Muslim policewomen don headscarves. *The Guardian.* https://www.theguardian.com/uk/2001/apr/25/ukcrime.religion

Kotecha, S. (2022, February 15). *Met police: Some officers are racist, professional standards chief admits.* https://www.bbc.com/news/uk-60379131

Laville, S. (2013, February 4). Senior Asian police officer retires after promotion snub over media skills. *The Guardian.* https://www.theguardian.com/uk/2013/feb/04/senior-asian-policeman-quits-met

Mayor of London. (2015, September 2016). *Met BME recruits more than double in first year of London only policy.* https://www.london.gov.uk/press-releases/mayoral/london-only-recruitment

McCulloh, A. (2017). Metropolitan police collars award for diversity and inclusion. *Personnel Today.* https://www.personneltoday.com/hr/personnel-today-awards-2017-award-diversity-inclusion/

Metropolitan Police. (2018). *2018 disclosure.* https://www.met.police.uk/foi-ai/metropolitan-police/disclosure-2018/september/all-london-mps-police-associations/?__cf_chl_captcha_tk__=pmd_xbQGXe8bB5GNjE3fq7IUJ5fU7S0NpBRC36U11P14UdI-1631187668-0-gqNtZGzNA2WjcnBszQjR

Metropolitan Police. (2021). STRIDE: *The Met's strategy for diversity, inclusion, and equity.* https://www.met.police.uk/SysSiteAssets/media/downloads/force-content/met/about-us/stride/strategy-for-inclusion-diversity-and-engagement-stride-2021-2025.pdf

ONS (Office of National Statistics). (2019, December 13). *Religion by sex and age-group in Great Britain, 2018 to 2019.* https://www.ons.gov.uk/peoplepopulationandcommunity/culturalidentity/religion/adhocs/10999religionbysexandagegroupingreatbritain2018to2019

Sal, R. (2000, November 12). Rasta recruits to the Met 'can wear their dreadlocks.' *The Telegraph.* https://www.telegraph.co.uk/news/uknews/1374117/Rasta-recruits-to-the-Met-can-wear-their-dreadlocks.html

The Irish Times. (2010, November 11). *50–50 PSNI recruitment to end.* https://www.irishtimes.com/news/50-50-psni-recruitment-to-end-1.867139

The Telegraph. (2010, April 22). *Sikh police banned from joining firearms teams wearing turbans.* https://www.telegraph.co.uk/news/uknews/law-and-order/7620128/Sikh-police-banned-from-joining-firearms-teams-wearing-turbans.html

Vertovec, S. (2007). Super-diversity and its implications. *Ethnic and Racial Studies, 30*(6), 1024–1054.

Weller, P., Feldman, A., & Purdam, K. (2001). *Religious discrimination in England and Wales: Home Office Research Study 220.* The Home Office.

CHAPTER 8

Understanding Religion, Culture, and the Role of Workplace Leadership in Nigeria

Abstract A complex relationship exists between religion and corporate cultures in societies with a high level of religious diversity. This chapter's case study of a Nigerian public sector organization explores the challenges of building a religiously inclusive workplace, highlighting the role of organizational leaders in shaping culture and embracing religious inclusion, and how the interplay of legal frameworks and national and corporate cultural contexts influences individual and group behaviors and outcomes in religiously diverse settings. There is evidence that progress can only be made when leaders are held accountable for assuring religious diversity in the workplace.

Keywords Religion and corporate culture · Diversity accountability · Cultural models · Religious accommodation · Nigeria

A little over ten years ago, a colleague of mine was in southern Nigeria for a retreat with a federal governmental agency. The retreat was slated to start early on Friday and end in the afternoon on Sunday, and employees from around Nigeria had been brought together to collaborate.

The retreat kicked off without a hitch at 8 a.m., but around noon, over a third of the delegates at the conference, including the Chief Financial

© The Author(s), under exclusive license to Springer Nature Switzerland AG 2022
E. Hasan, *Embracing Workplace Religious Diversity and Inclusion*, Palgrave Studies in Equity, Diversity, Inclusion, and Indigenization in Business, https://doi.org/10.1007/978-3-030-89773-4_8

Officer (CFO) left the retreat to pray. On Fridays, Muslims gather for a congregational prayer, and the participants at the retreat felt strongly that they must pray at a mosque with other Muslims. Though more than a third of the people at the retreat were Muslim, they only made up a quarter of the agency's employees. In all the planning that had gone into the retreat, no one had considered the needs of Muslim participants, possibly because they were a minority group at the company, and seemingly they hadn't been consulted. Not only were Friday prayers ignored—when at their home offices, it was typical for Muslim employees to take off three hours on Fridays for prayer—but also the fact that in southern Nigeria there are very few mosques, this wasn't even considered. Thus, the participants who took off on Friday couldn't just step out for their prayers. They had to travel a significant distance to find a mosque. As a solution, the federal agency abruptly decided that they would not continue the retreat on that day due to the number of attendees who had left for prayer.

Organizers had presumed that Muslim employees would ascribe to the cultural norms around retreats. In their minds, by having the retreat run from Friday through Sunday, Muslim employees would miss Friday prayer, and Christian employees would miss Sunday service. Because they were only asking for them to skip one religious observance for the year, and in support of a special retreat, the leadership team and organizers had thought it was a reasonable request. There was a feeling of exasperation as organizers wondered, *Why can't people sacrifice this one time? They can pray fifty-one other weekends of the year!* In reality, the fact that Muslim employees typically left for prayer on Fridays in a regular work week should have been acknowledged and factored into the decision-making surrounding the retreat.

Clearly, there was a disconnect between what the leadership team and organizers expected and what employees expected. And, because this was a federal governmental agency—unlike a private organization where everyone could have likely been fired on the spot—there was a greater impetus to accommodate the religious expression of employees.

It's a small moment of tension—one fairly easily resolved by shifting the schedule for the retreat—but this example of a workplace retreat coming into conflict with religious expression reveals the importance of examining and understanding our assumptions and biases about religion in the workplace.

CULTURAL MODELS, LEGAL FRAMEWORKS, AND RELIGION AT WORK

Any discussion of religion in public life is also a discussion of not just the legal frameworks, but the cultural context nationally, regionally, and in the workplace. While the existence of legal frameworks is more objective— though still ambiguous in interpretation in many cases as we've explored throughout this book—it is important to explore culture because it is not just the legislation of religious freedom that impacts the experiences of employees and employers. In fact, customs, traditions, and cultural norms greatly influence how religion and religious diversity and inclusion are treated by leaders, employees, and clients in the workplace.

We have explicitly explored at length the impact of legal frameworks on religious expression, religious freedom, and the public sphere, including the workplace thus far. By extension, but not always explicitly, we have also been discussing cultural norms and how they intersect with and influence religious expression and freedom. For instance:

- In Chapter 2, we explored the South African laws protecting the religious expression of Chef Mmoledi, making note of the way her supervisor's preference for the culturally acceptable Western doctor over the religious healer led to the courts ruling in her favor.
- In Chapter 5, we discussed both the legal frameworks protecting women who wear the hijab and the cultural norms around the hijab in the U.S., including exploring hijabophobia, Christian influence on cultural norms in American workplaces, and the culture identity of hijab-wearing women as a group.
- In Chapter 7, we looked at how the London Metropolitan Police Force was pushed to become more inclusive of ethnically and racially diverse officers and recruits by political and legal efforts and by the cultural expectations of the communities it serves.

As each of these examples demonstrate, culture has a significant influence on workplace religious inclusion.

Culture can be defined in a number of ways, as we discussed in Chapter 5, but for our purposes we can best understand culture as a powerful abstraction that consists of three levels: artifacts (i.e., language, clothing, and environment), espoused beliefs and values (i.e., philo-sophical views or ideologies), and basic underlying assumptions (i.e., unconscious beliefs or values) (Schein, 2004). As Gallimore and Goldenberg (2001) state, culture can be divided into two aspects: cultural models and cultural settings. A cultural model is the way we internalize our society's, community's, and family's assumptions about the world; a cultural setting is where we bring our cultural models. In other words, if a cultural model is the way people carry culture inside themselves, then a cultural setting is where cultural models are developed and lived. Looking at the example at the beginning of this chapter, we can identify two cultural models and one cultural setting: the Muslim cultural model, the Nigerian work cultural model, and the work retreat cultural setting.

The organizers, relying on the Nigerian work cultural model, assumed that because this event happened once a year and was an important retreat, it would take precedence over everything else, including religious expression. In a regular work week and with a governmental agency that has employees all over Nigeria, this cultural model was probably not regularly challenged. But when it came to a unique cultural setting, such as a retreat taking place over a weekend and outside typical work hours, the Muslim cultural model and the Nigerian work cultural model clashed, creating challenges for the Muslim employees who had to go against the grain to have their religious needs met and for the organizers who felt caught off guard by their needs. In this one moment, a national cultural model, a religious cultural model, and a workplace cultural setting all came together—what a compelling example of the nuance and complexity that comes into play when we discuss culture, religion, and the workplace.

To further understand these and other potential issues that come up in the workplace around culture and religion in Nigeria, it's important to have a sense of Nigeria's historical and contemporary relationship to religion.

Religion in Nigeria

Nigeria is a West African country with a remarkable amount of diversity. In fact, Nigeria is ranked as one of the five most diverse countries in the world (Adeleye et al., 2019; SHRM, 2009). It is also one of the most populous countries in the world with over 219 million people from more than 250 ethnolinguistic groups (Adeleye et al., 2019; CIA World Factbook, 2021). The Hausa-Fulani, Yoruba, and Igbo constitute the country's three largest ethnic groups, together comprising 66.7% of the population. Several other smaller ethnic groups are scattered across different parts of the country (CIA World Factbook, 2021).

Islam and Christianity are the main religions in the country, and both have an almost equal number of adherents; a small percentage of the population practice other religions including African indigenous religions (Adeleye et al., 2019; CIA World Factbook, 2021). Furthermore, it is not uncommon for a person to engage in the practice of more than one religious tradition to varying degrees (Harvard Divinity School, 2022). In comparison to its high ethnolinguistic diversity—the various forms of African indigenous religions practiced are vastly different—Nigeria's religious diversity at a cursory glance appears relatively low. Even though the population is almost evenly split between Christianity and Islam overall, the two religions are divided along geographical and ethnolinguistic lines. Muslims are concentrated in the Northern part of the country, which is made up of the Hausa-Fulani, while the South is predominantly Christian, and consists of the two other major tribes: the Yoruba and Igbo.

Nigeria's constitution, enacted in 1999, does not recognize any state religion, and explicitly prohibits any form of religious discrimination. That said, like many Africans, Nigerians are profoundly religious, and have many socio-cultural beliefs. Views on traditional gender roles in families and societies are deeply rooted in religion (Agbiji & Swart, 2015; Akinloye, 2018). In a 2006 PEW global study on religions, 76% of Christians and 91% of Muslims in Nigeria said their religion, rather than their nationality, ethnic group, or the African continent, was most important to them (Adeleye et al., 2019). Clearly, most Nigerians see religion as one of the most, if not the most, important aspects of their lives.

In Nigeria, religion is at the core of culture and can be infused into the very fabric of public life and the corporate culture of some organizations. Although many workers are well aware of this fusion of religion and corporate culture, the country's disparate economic profile and high unemployment levels—33.3% of the whole population and 42.5% of the large youth population (NBS, 2021)—leave few choices to those seeking employment.

Religion, Culture, and Conflict in Nigeria

There has been ongoing conflict in Nigeria for decades. Internally, Nigeria has displaced millions and produced over 300,000 refugees over the last decade (Operational Data Portal, 2022). Terrorist groups have targeted Muslims, Christians, oil workers, and corporations since 2011. Muslim-Christian conflict in the Middle Belt, the region that stretches across the center of Nigeria, has resulted in thousands of deaths since 2015 (USAID, 2019). Early 2019 was marked by election-related violence (European Asylum Support Office, 2021). State violence against terrorist groups has led to the deaths of many innocent civilians and that has created numerous refugees (Harvard Divinity School, 2022).

Despite the framing of this conflict in religious terms, more often than not it is a result of the unequal distribution of resources (Harvard Divinity School, 2022). That disparity has been related to religious and ethnic identity only to the degree that those identities have been leveraged by a powerful few to consolidate power and political influence in such a way that a small group has benefited while the majority are forced to compete for limited resources. At the same time, corruption is widespread (Harvard Divinity School, 2022). Furthermore, national economic policies have failed to stimulate growth and opportunity for most Nigerians, and conflict with religious overtones has continued as resources dwindle (Harvard Divinity School, 2022).

Increasing stratification across religious lines—and thus ethnic and regional lines as well—has become a serious threat to the stability of Nigeria. This ongoing conflict provides important context for how religious discrimination shows up in the workplace in a country with such high cultural and religious tensions.

Religious Discrimination and Culture

In countries with strong legal and institutional frameworks, citizens with religious discrimination cases can be somewhat confident the courts could deliver justice with minimal prejudice. In countries like Nigeria, where the legal frameworks are generally weak, that confidence is elusive. Workplace religious discrimination occurs more often than is formally reported; it is uncommon, in fact, for cases to be referred to courts or even for institutional agencies to receive such reports.

If an employee were to experience workplace religious discrimination in an environment with such a weak legal framework, they would have the option of reporting to the responsible authorities and ultimately seeking redress in court, if necessary. In countries where employment is difficult to secure and litigation is both timely and expensive, many would prefer to remain silent. One workplace discrimination case in which an employee was terminated because of her HIV status, for example, took over ten years to be adjudicated by the courts in Nigeria (Adeleye et al., 2019).

It's easy to see why many cases of workplace religious discrimination do not get the chance to be adjudicated by the courts. Given the economic situation and the high unemployment rates, many would rather choose to handle cases of workplace religious discrimination in alternative ways than risk losing their jobs or limit their chances of getting another. Therefore, there is little precedence of rulings regarding the few existing laws on religious discrimination in Nigeria.

THE ROLE OF THE LEADER IN MANAGING CULTURE AND RELIGION AT WORK

When a colleague traveled to Nigeria, he visited a federal transportation agency to gather data for a research project. While doing so, he observed a revealing phenomenon.

Two units on different floors inside the same building were observed, and stark differences jumped out immediately. One unit was filled with people who were Christian; they wore typical Western business attire like suits and ties, and they had degrees from Western universities and colleges. In many ways, that office looked like any office you might walk into in the West, though, of course, the whole staff was Nigerian. The second unit couldn't be more different from the first. In that unit, people were Muslim; they wore cultural attire including turbans and had prayer mats laid out in the office so they could easily engage in daily prayer.

When asked about the stark difference between the two units, a leader at the agency said that was just the way things work. Unit leaders have a good deal of autonomy, and if the head of a unit was Christian, they were more likely to hire employees who shared their Christian identity and values. If, instead, the head of a unit was Muslim, they would likely hire Muslim candidates to work with them.

This kind of bifurcation can start harmlessly enough. We all like to work with people who we think will understand us, value what we value, and respect our personal needs. So, in some ways, it makes sense to create teams with similar values. The issue arises when those groups continue to self-reinforce the inclusion of only people similar to the existing group. Over time that means that a federal research unit could be completely filled with Christian researchers who will make assumptions based on the

Christian cultural model about the way the world works. Even unintentionally, such intensive in-grouping leads to outcomes that aren't inclusive of everyone an organization serves.

This kind of issue comes up again and again in Nigeria. Despite being such a diverse country, very little attention is paid to IDE either nationally or in the workplace. Part of this can be attributed to the regional differences in Nigeria; as you'll remember from above, there are very few places that people of different religious identities come together other than a few cosmopolitan cities like Lagos. Due to this geographical concentration, religious IDE just hasn't gained prominence.

At the same time, as we've seen with two different examples from federal agencies, ignoring religious diversity and inclusion can lead to conflict, oversight, and religious exclusion, all of which can undermine the business efforts of an organization. These factors make it clear that the onus for creating equal and inclusive experiences for all religiously diverse workers is on employers and leaders.

Leaders, from the C suite to HR to IDE professionals to managers, can have a significant impact on workplace religious diversity and inclusion, as we have discussed throughout this book. At the same time, these leaders can also be a part of the problem. When leaders avoid the topic of religion by refusing to have explicit policies about religious expression, attire, holidays, and prayer options, they leave too much room for interpretation, disagreement, and unfortunately, discrimination. In national contexts like in Nigeria where there is a weak legal framework and no equivalent of the EEOC in the U.S., leaders can bridge the gap between the nation and workplace by articulating what the organization stands for, what their policies are, and what religious diversity and inclusion look like. Furthermore, leaders and organizations can articulate the organization's religious IDE agenda explicitly and in writing so that there is more clarity and less confusion about the role of religion and culture in the workplace.

It is apparent that religious beliefs and cultural norms have influence on both strategic and operational decisions in corporate organizations. An organization could have clear, formal values and policies but still be managed by the individual values and beliefs of its top management, leading some corporate cultures to be overtly infused with religion because of the support of top management for a particular religion. So, in managing religious diversity, merely having formally stated core values and policies—while necessary—may not be enough to create religious inclusion. Securing leadership commitment is vital for organizations to create and sustain a culture of inclusion.

Research has already stressed the role of organizational leadership in managing diversity. When an organization's top leadership supports diversity, employees will usually follow suit (Rahman, 2019). Indeed, the stance of top leadership generally influences the climate and corporate culture of organizations. Furthermore, management, not just the workforce, needs to be religiously diverse enough to serve the interest of a religiously diverse workforce and create an inclusive workplace free of discrimination (Ashikali et al., 2021).

As a leader of an organization, you have an opportunity to help your workplace become more inclusive and less biased. The truth is that we all have unconscious biases—stereotypes of certain groups of people that we form outside of our awareness—and we all make assumptions. In fact, this is a key function of the human brain: to sort large amounts of input rapidly into digestible information, paying special attention to anything that seems dangerous. As we gather that information, we begin to form mental shortcuts. Quinetta Roberson, Professor of Management and Psychology at Michigan State University, defines these shortcuts as quick, routine, and reactive responses driven by our instincts that help us fill in the blanks in familiar scenarios (2020).

When it comes to people, Roberson argues, we categorize individuals into social groups such as gender, race, ethnicity, or even alma mater. This process helps us identify where we fit in our environment and how we relate to those around us. It even makes us feel good about who we are. However, when we encounter someone we don't know or have enough information for, our shortcuts activate and our brains fill in the details of who someone is. If that image we've constructed is broken—if say, a woman who wears a hijab says that she loves her hijab in an American cultural context and that counters what a Christian believes about women who wear the hijab—we may reject that information, or we can internalize that information and recalibrate. In fact, this is how we overcome bias.

As a leader, it's your job not only to overcome your own bias, unconscious or not, but to also help your staff overcome their own as well. Here are some ways Robinson has identified that you can work to overcome bias in the workplace (2019):

- Create opportunities for employees to find common ground. When people connect across religious identities about shared interests like hobbies, they begin to see each other as individuals, rather than categories. Yukio sees Miriam as a fellow marathoner and a Jewish person, rather than an unknown Jewish person, and this creates a two-dimensional identity. We also see how much in common we have, even though we may have much that makes us different as well.

- Invite your employees to share who they are. Adopt a curious mindset about your employees and their religious identities, asking them questions about their lives. Not only will this help you get to know who your employees are on a real level, but it will also help you model healthy curiosity for your other employees. If you're interested in learning more about mindset, make sure to read the next chapter where we'll explore that concept further.
- Embrace not-knowing. It's ok to be surprised about the religious identity or expression of a colleague. Help your employees realize they don't have to pretend they know everything, and that they can instead learn something new without feeling threatened.
- When you make mistakes, internalize the lesson. When we live and work in diverse environments, we're bound to make mistakes with one another. It's important to apologize when we hurt someone, of course, but it's all the more important to internalize the lesson and let your mental shortcuts shift and change.
- Sit with discomfort. When we receive information we don't know how to sort, it makes us feel uncomfortable, which is actually a sign that you're on the right path. The next time someone challenges your way of thinking about the world, take a moment to realize the unique experience you get in meeting this person, and try to be grateful for their perspective even if you don't agree.

There are two additional ways to overcome bias that I would like to add to Roberson's insights:

- Embrace the moral case for religious inclusion. As we discussed in Chapter 2, proactively managing religious diversity and inclusion shows a respect for the freedoms of thought and expression, important features of the modern workplace, and allows organizations to tap into the motivations of religiously diverse employees to inspire their best work.

- Identify and acknowledge your own cultural models. We each come to the workplace with cultural models, and those models change the way the workplace functions, particularly, when leaders have strong, unacknowledged cultural models. When those models are based on something so integral to one's identity as religion, then they can become cemented and unaccommodating of other people's religious cultural models. That's why it's so important to be curious about others, as we'll discuss in Chapter 10.

While all of these strategies work across identities, these kinds of connections and forging new mental pathways can be particularly helpful when it comes to the religious cultural models leaders and employees bring to the workplace.

In the final analysis, leaders are faced with the task of preventing their personal religious cultural model from influencing their decision-making and ensuring that formal policies are always followed. Compliance with this form of professionalism is an undertaking that is difficult to enforce especially in institutionally and legally weak contexts. Knowledgeable and courageous HR professionals may be needed to act as change agents to drive religious diversity and inclusion (Adeleye et al., 2019).

Assessing the Level of Religious Inclusion in Nigeria

The discussion of religious inclusion in Nigeria looks a little different than it has in other chapters. In this chapter we've explored how cultural models and cultural norms influence the workplace, particularly around religious diversity and inclusion. We've talked about cultural norms around IDE, the geographical concentration of religious identities, and the realities of Nigerian workplace cultural settings. Despite the irregularity of this chapter, the Kaizen HC Model of Religious Inclusion can be utilized.

The organizations we've discussed in Nigeria are decidedly at Level 1: Avoidance. Discussions of IDE, and religious diversity and inclusion in particular are rare in the workplace. As we saw with the federal transportation agency, the religious identity of leaders may hold great sway over who is hired at their unit or organization, which might make you think it's approaching Level 3: Emerging. I would argue that while religion is influencing who is hired, it isn't acknowledged, understood, or explicitly supported. It's an example of a cultural model based loosely on a religious identity holding sway over a cultural setting.

For organizations like the governmental agencies discussed in this chapter to move into Level 2: Compliance, there would have to be some sort of national legislation regarding religious freedoms, and the formation of an organization like the EEOC to administer and enforce those laws in the workplace. Additionally, organizations would need to become familiar with and invested in the legal, business, and moral cases for religious inclusion and belonging.

All organizations exist not just inside cultural contexts, but also inside legal frameworks that prohibit and require certain activities of employers. As we explored in Chapter 2, how the right to religious freedom is protected in legislation and how those laws are interpreted varies greatly. In the following chapter, we'll explore Australia's new religious freedom bill, as well as the role of leaders and the qualities you can harness to become a more inclusive leader, using a different national and legal context to explore these qualities.

REFERENCES

Adeleye, I., Fawehinmi, A., Adisa, T., Kingsley Utam, K. & Ikechukwu-Ifudu, V. (2019). Managing diversity in Nigeria: Competing Logics of workplace diversity. In A. Georgiadou, M. Alejandra Gonzalez-Perez, & M. R. Olivas-Luján (Eds.), *Diversity within diversity management (Advanced series in management)* (Vol. 21, pp. 21–40). Emerald Publishing Limited.
Agbiji, O. M., & Swart, I. (2015). Religion and social transformation in Africa: A critical and appreciative perspective. *Scriptura, 114*, 1–20.
Akinloye, I. A. (2018). Towards the implementation of sustainable development goals in Nigeria: Maximizing the influence of religious leaders. *Stellenbosch Theological Journal, 4*(1), 39–60. https://doi.org/10.7833/114-0-1115
Ashikali, T., Groeneveld, S., & Kuipers, B. (2021). The role of inclusive leadership in supporting an inclusive climate in diverse public sector teams. *Review of Public Personnel Administration, 41*(3), 497–519.
CIA World Factbook. (2021). *Nigeria.* https://www.cia.gov/the-world-factbook/countries/nigeria/#people-and-society
European Asylum Support Office. (2021). *Nigeria security situation.* https://www.justice.gov/eoir/page/file/1405116/download

Gallimore, R., & Goldenberg, C. (2001). Analyzing cultural models and settings to connect minority achievement and school improvement research. *Educational Psychologist, 36*(1), 45–56. https://doi.org/10.1207/S15326985EP3 601_5

Harvard Divinity School. (2022). *Religion and public life: Nigeria.* https://rpl. hds.harvard.edu/religion-context/country-profiles/nigeria

NBS. (2021). *Unemployment statistics.* https://nigerianstat.gov.ng/

Operational Data Portal. (2022). *Regional response: Nigeria situation.* https:// data2.unhcr.org/en/situations/nigeriasituation#_ga=2.158750778.187 47392.1594052076-1302264614.1593548152

Rahman, U. H. F. B. (2019). Diversity management and the role of leader. *Open Economics, 2*, 30–39. https://doi.org/10.1515/openec-2019-0003/html?lan g=en

Roberson, Q. (2020). The other side of bias. *TEDxUniversityofDelaware.* https://www.youtube.com/watch?v=H2vvYmEZaNk

Schein, E. H. (2004). *Organizational culture and leadership* (3rd ed.). Jossey-Bass.

SHRM. (2009). Global diversity and inclusion: Perceptions, practices and attitudes. *Society for human resource management.* SHRM.

USAID. (2019). *USAID's conflict mitigation activity promotes peaceful coexistence between middle belt farmers and herders.* https://www.usaid.gov/nig eria/press-releases/may-23-2019-usaid%E2%80%99s-conflict-mitigation-act ivity-promotes-peaceful

CHAPTER 9

Yearning for Religious Freedom in Australia

Abstract There has been a fierce debate in recent years about the role of religion in society and the workplace. In the Western world, this debate is evident in national politics and the so-called culture wars. Australia provides an interesting context to explore this issue. Following the firing of a Christian rugby star for homophobic comments made on social media in 2018, the Australian government proposed legislative changes to protect religious freedom. This chapter provides an analysis of the potential impact of such laws, and highlights the challenges and limitations of a compliance-focused approach to religious inclusion.

Keywords Religious freedom · Religious anti-discrimination laws · Australian politics · LGBTQ+ · Inclusion

In April 2019, an Australian rugby union player named Israel Folau made a homophobic post on social media, which led to his employer firing him. Folau cited being a devout Christian as the basis for his statement and sued his employer Rugby Australian and the New South Wales Waratahs Club for unfair dismissal (Packham, 2019). In late 2019, Rugby Australia issued an apology, and the parties settled out of court.

E. Hasan, *Embracing Workplace Religious Diversity and Inclusion*, Palgrave Studies in Equity, Diversity, Inclusion, and Indigenization in Business, https://doi.org/10.1007/978-3-030-89773-4_9

While these events triggered a heated, nationwide debate about the freedom of speech and religion, there was already a great deal of concern about religious inclusion in Australia. In recent years, mosques and synagogues have been vandalized (Kohn, 2020; Powell, 2019); in some cases, swastikas were painted over religious symbols and in others, the name of the Christchurch shooter from neighboring New Zealand was scrawled on buildings. Women who wear the hijab in Australia have also reported experiencing a good deal of abuse and violence, according to a study from Charles Sturt University (Iner, 2019).

These alarming incidents and the high-profile firing of Folau have ultimately resulted in new proposed legislation to protect religious expression with a focus on people who express their religion outside of work. Australia's Attorney-General, Christian Porter, contends the proposed legislation—referred to as the Religious Discrimination Bill of 2019— would allow Australians to express their religious views in the workplace. Opponents, including Australia's Human Rights Law Centre, have raised concerns that the bill is unbalanced and does not adequately consider the right to equality. LGBTQ+ and human rights groups believe the bill enables people to express bigoted views and derogatory—even harmful— comments in the public sphere (BBC, 2021). The proposed legislation also addresses the role of religion in the workplace and issues of workplace religious discrimination.

Public reactions to the first draft of the proposed legislation have unearthed long-standing tensions, revealing Australia's deep historical divide along religious lines. Some Australians agree that more specific legislation on religious freedom and discrimination is needed, while others contend that the law is sufficient, citing the outcome of Folau's case—he did, after all, receive an apology and a settlement from Rugby Australia (Equality Australia, 2019).

Legislation directly addressing religion and religious freedom appears in the commonwealth constitution and international treaties and conventions signed by Australia. These include the International Covenant on Civil and Political Rights (ICCPR), Convention on the Elimination of all forms of Racial Discrimination (CERD), and Convention of the Rights of the Child (CRC). Section 116 of Australia's constitution prohibits the making of any law "establishing any religion, or for imposing any religious observance, or for prohibiting the free exercise of any religion," and prohibits the use of religious tests as a requirement into public office or trust. States within Australia also have different legislation prohibiting religious and other forms of discrimination. Despite these provisions, the history of Australia shows that religion seems to have played a prominent role in public life in the country.

As we discussed in Chapter 2, it is the interpretation of existing laws that matter rather than the laws themselves. Australian courts have generally interpreted the provision of section 116 of the commonwealth constitution as a limitation of the powers of the government to establish a state religion rather than a freestanding right for all Australians (Cruickshank, 2021).

Therefore, the government's current attempt to promote specific legislation on religion and religious freedom may be set to change, or at least make clearer, the role of religion in public life. The government's decision itself is an acknowledgment of increasing diversity and growing religious pluralism in Australian society.

Australia's current exploration of new legislation and public discourse regarding religion in public life demonstrates that legislating for religious freedom is not a simple task. It requires acknowledging the many types of freedom in question and ensuring religious freedom does not mean exclusion of other groups.

RELIGION IN AUSTRALIA

Historically, Australia has always been very diverse, a fact that may not be readily apparent to those unfamiliar with the nation. The indigenous peoples of Australia have 50,000 years of historical diversity; during that time and contemporarily, over 250 languages and 600 dialects have been spoken. Today, the indigenous peoples of Australia comprise less than 2% of the country's population (Bouma & Halafoff, 2017).

Before the immigration restriction Act of 1901, popularly referred to as the "white Australia policy," people of diverse religions arrived in the country to work in the plantations and goldmines (Ganter, 2008). But post 1901, religious pluralism became pluralism in Christian denominations, and religious freedom implicitly referred to the freedom to choose between the different denominations. In 1911, Christians constituted about 96.9% of the population, the majority of them having affiliations with either the Roman Catholic Church or the Anglican Church of Australia. Different migration patterns have since changed the religious landscape.

Increasingly, Australians are ascribing to non-Christian religions, and about one third of the population now identify with no religion. In fact, 2016 census figures from the Australian Bureau of Statistics reveal:

- Most (22.6%) Australians who affiliate with a religion are Roman Catholics. There are over five million people who are Roman Catholic in Australia.
- Anglicans make up the next largest group with over three million adherents who make up 13.3% of the population.
- Seven groups make up between around two and four percent of the population: Uniting Church Christians (3.7%), Muslims (2.6%), Buddhists (2.4%), Presbyterian and Reformed Church Christians (2.3%), and Hindus (1.9%).
- Four more groups each make up 1.5% of the population or less: Baptist Church Christians (1.5%), Pentecostal Church Christians (1.1%), Sikhs (0.5%), and Jews (0.4%).
- People who are unaffiliated—those who did not report a religion or who may be agnostics, atheists, and so on—make up 47.7% of the population. There are over eleven million people who belong to this group, more than doubling the next largest group, the Roman Catholics.

This census data reveals Australia to be much more diverse than generally acknowledged.

In fact, we could use the term superdiversity, which we explored in Chapter 7, to describe Australia. Australia may not be as super diverse as the UK, for which the term was coined, but its high level of diversity, particularly religious diversity, is indisputable. This high diversity, coupled with Australia having no officially recognized state religion, gives the impression that there is significant religious freedom in the country, but there are other influential factors that have formed the landscape. Historically, Australia as a country was governed by British colonists who were largely influenced by Western Christianity, culture, political structures, and institutions, particularly from the Church of England. Political power rested with the Christian majority, and they influenced policies to the extent that welfare policies were administered by churches on behalf of the state, and aid was sometimes provided to some church denominations (Cruickshank, 2021). Governmental financial aid was also provided to many private schools that were mostly owned by Christian denominations such as the Roman Catholic Church.

Although the government has taken a stance of religious neutrality in recent times, this historical precedence of the beneficial relationship between the church and the state still has some influence on the perception of the government's official position regarding religion. Indeed, it is still serving as a barrier to the formation of religious freedom laws. Recent grants and financial aid provided by state governments to some faith communities in response to the COVID-19 pandemic further supports those who believe the government is biased in favor of religious people and institutions, predominantly Christians (McGrath et al., 2021).

This perception is reflected in the divergent views in the public's responses on the first draft of the new legislation on religious freedom. Some still perceive the government as showing favoritism to Christians above adherents of other religions despite the increased religious diversity. Others perceive the government as trying to stifle the freedom of the Christian majority. Some worry the right to equality will be trumped by the right to freedom of religion. These divergent views reveal hidden historical religious tensions.

Public Review of the Religious Discrimination Bill

In early 2020, the second draft of the Religious Discrimination Bill of 2019 was released for public review and feedback-gathering. The new draft makes provisions for certain religious bodies to make decisions in alignment with their religious beliefs. The bill's definition of religious bodies, though, extends beyond traditional boundary definitions to include all bodies with religious beliefs, except hospitals and accommodation providers who do not engage in solely or primarily commercial activities. From this definition, educational institutions such as schools and universities owned by religious organizations are considered to be religious bodies and can give preference to persons of the same religion in conducting their activities. The bill aims to protect religious bodies against the threat of discrimination claims in instances where a religious body is acting in accordance with its religious beliefs (McLuckie & Ford, 2020). The draft bill also provides protection for individuals of faith against discrimination on the basis of their religious beliefs and practices in certain areas of public life.

Under the proposed laws, large businesses with turnover above AU$50 million (approximately $38.6 million USD) will be banned from having policies that prohibit or restrict employees from making statements of beliefs outside working hours, unless employers can prove that such statements would cause unjustifiable financial hardship on their business. Effectively, this specific provision provides freedom for workers to express their religious beliefs and to effectively practice their religion outside the workplace as long as it does not infringe on the rights of others.

These and other provisions in the bill have provoked a myriad of public reactions from Australians. Over 7,000 submissions on the second draft of the bill were received by the government (U.S. Department of State, 2021). Some argue that the religious discrimination bill provides too much liberty to religious Australians, especially implicitly to the Christian majority, and does not provide enough protection for the human rights of minority groups. Others argue that the provisions of the bill do not provide enough religious freedom and it impedes the religious practices of certain religious groups.

Regarding protecting the human rights of minority groups, there are several concerns about the proposed legislation; chief among them is that the protection seems to be coming at the expense of other rights, which can be regarded as providing excessive protection to religious persons and bodies. Other concerns include:

- Current provisions could prevent members of minority groups such as LGBTQ+ from participating in some economic sectors in Australia as the bill gives protection to religious bodies and organizations that refuse to offer goods and services to certain minority groups. This potential for excluding minority groups from participating in the economy is considered discriminatory.
- Some provisions of the bill also provide room for discriminatory comments against minority groups.
- Some provisions relating to expression of religious beliefs and practices in the workplace create difficulty for nonreligious and private sector employers who want to create a balanced and inclusive workplace for all employees.

Addressing the issues raised will serve to improve the bill. While the rights to the expression of religious beliefs and practices should be protected, they should not impede on the rights of others.

Despite sharing similar concerns on either side of the divide, there is no seamless unity among the two camps. Neither side can be exclusively linked to one religious group or the other, or even to the religiously affiliated and those who are not. Neither side is completely against or in total support of the bill. Both sides have acknowledged that creating the perfect religious freedom legislation—one that completely satisfies the desires and aspirations of all Australians while simultaneously protecting the rights of all—is out of reach. The challenge then is to write legislation that is mutually beneficial to both sides while leaving a small enough room for the courts to provide arbitration on any excluded areas when and where necessary. Harmonizing the varied public opinions shared in response to the legislation drafts remains the major task of the government if the bill is to make progress toward becoming the legal framework for religious discrimination in Australia.

In November 2021, a third draft of the religious discrimination bill was released with Prime Minister Scott Morrison hoping to see the bill introduced before the end of the year (The Conversation, 2021). While the fate of the bill is unclear, and further debate is ongoing, some pertinent questions are raised. How can the government harmonize the views of all religious groups and minority groups that may not have any religious affiliation? Although the bill is meant to go beyond religious discrimination in the workplace to the wider society, its effects on organizations and employers remain unclear: How does the bill affect the definition of workplace religious discrimination in Australia? Perhaps, the most crucial question of all is, Does the government's aim to protect religious freedom and fight against religious discrimination come at the expense of minorities and those without religious affiliation?

POTENTIAL IMPACTS ON WORKPLACE RELIGIOUS DIVERSITY AND INCLUSION

Only time will tell how these questions are answered in Australia, though they are illuminating questions both for policymakers in other countries and regions considering religious discrimination legislation, as well as for people working in contexts with strong, specific legal frameworks regarding religious diversity and discrimination.

As we have seen in Australia, the interconnected nature of culture, history, law, and politics have far-reaching effects on legislation and how legal provisions are understood and interpreted. The effects of these factors, however, are often neither obvious nor clear-cut. Consequently, the provisions in legal frameworks for religious freedom, and against religious discrimination, may be prejudiced depending on the interplay of these factors. Even how various terms are defined can lead to surprising outcomes. For instance, if the religious freedom bill becomes legislation as it is now, religious bodies in Australia would include schools, charities, and other commercial organizations involved in the production of goods and rendering of services that would otherwise be regarded as private organizations in other countries. It is clear that when it comes to understanding and managing workplace religious diversity, the importance of legislation and legal frameworks cannot be over emphasized, as we discussed in Chapter 2.

Despite the unique situational factors, the yearning for religious freedom in Australia is not particularly unusual. Freedom of religion and freedom of speech are fundamental rights of every person. The challenge of legislation lies in knowing where to place the boundaries around the granting of religious freedom and expression to a person or group to avoid infringing on the fundamental rights of others. The expression of the religious beliefs of some major religious groups, for example, could infringe on the rights of some minority groups such as LGBTQ+ people who are also entitled to their fundamental human rights.

How Religious Freedom Laws Impact Workplaces, Employers, and Employees

When considering the workplace, the management of religious diversity and inclusion, necessarily, requires acknowledging and managing the tensions between groups of people that may reflect fissures in wider society. It is understandable that this task may seem overwhelming. Here are some of the considerations, both within and outside an organization's control, that will influence this process:

- Legal frameworks. As this chapter has explored at length, it is not just what the legislation states, but how it is interpreted that will influence its impact on the workplace. Ideally, legislation needs to be stated in a balanced way, free from any specific controversy or perceived bias toward any group; as Australia has shown, that is rarely the case.

- Public vs. private. The way the current draft of Australia's religious discrimination bill is stated, it makes it clear that there are private, religious bodies that have different rules than public institutions. While that provision may revolutionize how some of these organizations, including schools, are viewed, it also reveals potentially impactful differences between public and private institutions in regard to religious freedom.
- Majority vs. minority. Protecting the rights of religious minorities and historically excluded religious groups should be the priority of any organization. As it stands, religious freedom laws can sometimes protect the declining influence or concerns of the religious majority. Even if the government doesn't prioritize minority groups, organizations that focus on belonging and inclusion will.

These factors should be at the front of the mind for any organization as it decides how to bring religion into the workplace. Furthermore, legislators should be aware not just of these factors, but of the current developments in Australia and other nations considering religious discrimination laws.

The government of Australia is grappling with harmonizing the yearning for more religious freedom with the human rights of many minorities, trying to accommodate everyone. Dropping the religious freedom bill entirely no longer seems to be an option, particularly given Prime Minister Scott Morrison's support of it. It is understood, however, that the bill must include provisions that are satisfactory to both sides. The courts are there to provide interpretation and jurisdiction in particular situations that will inevitably occur if and when the bill passes to become law.

As with the last chapter, the truth is that religious freedom laws, like cultural norms, are well outside of the control of any organization or leader. That said, there's still a lot of room to explore how leaders can help drive more inclusive workplace cultures. While it's tempting to focus on small changes you can make, organizations and leaders must explore the root causes of workplace religious discrimination, and not just look at the symptoms. Symptoms can range from failed recruitment efforts to low retention of religiously diverse employees to conflict between employees. These are all matters that might seem to have simple solutions, but if the underlying causes aren't addressed, any solution will be temporary. When we explore the root causes, such as societal and cultural norms, industry demands, and the values and beliefs of leadership, it becomes clear that the work that lies before us starts with individual people (Bauer & Erdogan, 2010).

It can be hard to hear, but in many cases, leaders, from CEOs to HR professionals to managers, can often become a part of the problem by ignoring religion wholesale or only supporting the expression of one's own religious traditions. When religion is avoided in official policies and communication, it sends a very clear message that there are no protections for religious people, and this encourages employees to engage in hiding their diverse religious identities. Rather than ignoring religion—and national conversations about religious freedom like those taking place in Australia—savvy leaders can use those conversations to help their organization become more responsive to their religiously diverse employees and customers.

Assessing the Level of Religious Inclusion in Australia

Religious inclusion in Australia deviates from other case studies—here we explore how policymakers are pushing for new legislation regarding religious freedom, rather than exploring a unique workplace scenario. That said, the Kaizen HC Model of Religious Inclusion can still be utilized to evaluate legal frameworks.

Australia is at Level 2: Compliance. They are no longer avoiding religious diversity and inclusion and in fact, they're focused on making religious freedom more explicit in legislation. Policymakers are attempting to protect their stakeholders from lawsuits and adverse legal decisions. That said, the legislation itself and the policymakers advocating for it could be seen to have too narrow a focus on one dominant religion rather than on protecting the freedom of all religious expression and none. Policymakers seem to have various motivations for supporting the bill, though there has been little discussion of religious inclusion and belonging for all.

Moving forward, the legislation will have to account not only for protecting the declining influence of the religious majority but also for the rights of the historically excluded—including the indigenous peoples and other minorities (e.g., Muslims and Sikhs).

The legislation and debate regarding religious freedom could have major ramifications for employees and workplaces in Australia. As the global trends we discussed in Chapter 3 continue to bring religiously diverse people into contact with one another, similar conversations and legislation may arise.

Each of the scenarios from around the world that we've examined illustrates the complexity of workplaces today and provides a foundation as we look to the future of workplace religious diversity and inclusion. In the next chapter, we'll explore what the future holds and how we can each become better advocates for religious IDE.

REFERENCES

Australian Bureau of Statistics. (2016). *2016 census*. https://www.abs.gov.au/websitedbs/censushome.nsf/home/2016

Bauer, T., & Erdogan, B. (2010). *An introduction to Organization Culture* (2nd ed.). Flat World Knowledge Inc.

BBC. (2021, November 25). *Australia: LGBTQ advocates blast religious discrimination bill*. https://www.bbc.com/news/world-australia-59411999

Bouma, G. D., & Halafoff, A. (2017). Australia's changing religious profile - Rising Nones and Pentecostals, declining British Protestants in Superdiversity: Views from the 2016 Census. *Journal for the Academic Study of Religion, 30*(2), 129–143. https://doi.org/10.1558/jasr.34826

Cruickshank, J. (2021). Religious freedom in 'the most godless place under heaven': Making policy for religion in Australia. *History Australia, 18*(1), 42–52. https://doi.org/10.1080/14490854.2021.1878466

Equality Australia. (2019, December 4). *Settlement between Rugby Australia and Israel Folau shows that there is no need for new religious discrimination law*. https://equalityaustralia.org.au/folau-settlement/

Ganter, R. (2008). Muslim Australians: The deep histories of contact. *Journal of Australian Studies, 32*(4), 481–492. https://doi.org/10.1080/14443050802471384

Iner, D. (2019). Islamophobia in Australia II: 2016–2017. *Islamophobia Register Australia*. http://www.islamophobia.com.au/resources/

Kohn, P. (2020, January 23). Vandalism at shule. *The Australian Jewish News*. https://www.australianjewishnews.com/vandalism-at-shule/

McGrath, P., King, T., & Smiley, M. (2021, August 4). Churches, religious groups received millions of dollars in JobKeeper while staying in the black, accounts show. *ABC News*. https://www.abc.net.au/news/2021-08-05/churches-religious-entities-got-millions-in-jobkeeper-payments/100349412

McLuckie, S., & Ford, D. (2020). Australia: Religious freedom legislation. *Mondaq*. https://www.mondaq.com/australia/human-rights/899830/religious-freedom-legislation

Packham, C. (2019, August 29). Australia unveils religious freedom bill, after rugby star sacked for 'hell awaits homosexuals' post. *Reuters*. https://www.reuters.com/article/us-australia-religion/australia-unveils-religious-freedom-bill-after-rugby-star-sacked-for-hell-awaits-homosexuals-post-idUSKCN1V J0MC

Powell, R. (2019, September 11). Brisbane's Holland Park mosque vandalised with swastika, accused Christchurch shooter's name on walls. *ABC News*. https://www.abc.net.au/news/2019-09-11/brisbane-mosque-vandalised-with-christchurch-references/11501684

The Conversation. (2021, November 23). *Third time lucky? What has changed in the latest draft of the religious discrimination bill?* https://theconversation.com/third-time-lucky-what-has-changed-in-the-latest-draft-of-the-religious-discrimination-bill-172386

U.S. Department of State. (2021). *2020 report on international religious freedom: Australia*. https://www.state.gov/reports/2020-report-on-international-religious-freedom/australia/

The Future of Workplace Religious Diversity and Inclusion: Opportunities, Challenges, and Recommendations

Abstract This concluding chapter reiterates the importance of embracing workplace religious inclusion. This is a rational decision in a world where the continued growth of religious populations and religious diversity is predicted for the next three decades or so. Embracing religious inclusion poses many challenges, but these are not insurmountable. Getting workplace religious diversity and inclusion right requires a culture of joint accountability for outcomes. The chapter discusses the role of policy makers, business leaders, organizational researchers—everyone—in building safe and religiously inclusive workplaces and societies.

Keywords Kaizen HC model of religious inclusion · Religious discrimination lawsuit · Religious Equity Diversity and Inclusion (REDI) Index · Inclusive leadership · Workplace culture

In 2010, over 83% of the global population affiliated with a religion (PEW Research, 2015). This rate is projected to increase to 86.8% in 2050, leaving a mere 13.2% of the total world population not affiliating with any religion. These statistics and numerous examples throughout this book make it clear that religious diversity isn't going anywhere—in fact, the world is getting more religious, and more religiously diverse. The number

© The Author(s), under exclusive license to Springer Nature
Switzerland AG 2022
E. Hasan, *Embracing Workplace Religious Diversity and Inclusion*,
Palgrave Studies in Equity, Diversity, Inclusion, and Indigenization
in Business, https://doi.org/10.1007/978-3-030-89773-4_10

of people projected to be Muslim, for example, will be almost at par with the number of Christians by 2050 (PEW Research, 2015).

At a time when religion is on the rise and continues to rise, restrictions have also risen. These restrictions on religion globally—discussed at length in Chapter 3—such as governments' limits on religious activities and harassment of religious groups, hostilities toward some religious norms and practices, and organized violence against religious groups have increased the world over, with an alarming rise in restrictions rippling through Europe (Diamont, 2019).

In recognition of these dual realities, religious inclusion and belonging must be a focus of organizational leaders, policymakers, and everyone who works and lives in diversifying societies. Not only do inclusion and belonging lead to safer, better workplaces for all workers, but they also enhance organizational performance. Just as importantly, organizations will need to be more inclusive to avoid engaging in discrimination.

There has already been a rapid rise in the number of cases of alleged religious discrimination in the U.S., Europe, and Western countries in general. In less developed countries, where there seem to be fewer formal reports of religious discrimination allegations, the data and the reality may diverge greatly, as we saw in Chapter 9.

In the U.S., EEOC data shows that in 1997, 1,709 cases of alleged religious discrimination were received by the commission. By 2008, this number had increased to 3,273 and to 4,151 in 2011. Overall, increase in the number of charges of religious discrimination received by the commission between 1997 and 2020 was 41% (EEOC, 2021). Monetary benefits received by complainants totaled over $187.4 million over the years between 1997 and 2020 (EEOC, 2021); this figure excludes the amount of money paid out in respect of litigation cases. The simple truth is that organizations can no longer afford to neglect their religious diversity.

Costs are also not limited to monetary terms. Failure to manage or ineffective management of religious diversity could lead to costly losses due to workplace conflict, lost productivity, and erosion of the brand image. Cases and allegations of religious discrimination are likely to continue to increase, not only in the U.S., but in other Western countries also. Countries in Africa, Latin America, and in parts of Asia that have not seen court cases regarding religious discrimination up to this point are likely to begin seeing some as their religious diversity and level of development increase. The only exceptions are in countries with extreme levels of restrictions on religions, and those where state religions are likely to still hold sway. Therefore, organizations and countries need to take religious diversity more seriously. Recent legal and cultural discourse in countries such as Australia, France, and some European countries show the complexities that can arise in trying to manage religious diversity; neglecting the issue is no longer an option.

WHAT CAN POLICYMAKERS DO?

As religious diversity increases in the U.S., we expect to see more cases of religious discrimination filed at the EEOC. While the number of successful cases is expected to remain relatively low, per historical trends, policymakers and employers alike need to take a proactive stand to managing religious diversity (EEOC, 2021). We expect to see two key patterns in the U.S. First, the religious right, also known as the political far right, will likely engage more deeply in the fight for more religious freedom to protect the rights and dominance of the Christian majority in the workplace; this would likely lead to polarizing legal challenges and court battles. Second, Muslims, Jews, Sikhs, other religious minorities, and their allies will likely increase their activism and advocacy, particularly as these groups become more mainstream in American society. What remains elusive is the idea of both religious majority and minorities combining forces to push for more religious accommodations and religious inclusion in the workplace.

Outside the U.S., for example in France and the EU, the secularization of society is likely to advance. Religious minorities and majorities are likely to face secular laws that emphasize neutrality and object to blatantly religious external/physical appearances. If religious inclusion advocates are able to make a strong business and moral case for their cause, a two-way track may emerge with laws remaining secular while forward-thinking organizations embrace religious inclusion within their workplace and beyond. As we've seen with progress on race and gender diversity, when organizations take the lead in tackling discrimination and inequity in response to stakeholder pressure or for business reasons, that's when change happens. So, change is possible even without a supportive legal environment.

As globalization and migration across national boundaries continue—as we explored in Chapter 3—more countries are going to become more religiously diverse in the future. We have seen from the case of Australia in Chapter 7 that legislating religion and matters of religious discrimination are not so simple. So, the solution is not simply enacting legislation. Neither is placing more restrictions on religion in various forms necessarily the solution.

A good starting point could be having strong legislative and legal frameworks that recognize and accommodate the fundamental rights of all. In this regard, either including specific provisions in existing general legislation or having specific legislation dedicated to religion and religious discrimination matters are viable options. In either option, a clear absence of bias and the political will to ensure that all people, regardless of their religious beliefs, feel included are paramount.

Perception is a crucial component of this work. People of different religious beliefs, and those with no religious belief, need to believe the government aims to protect the fundamental and religious rights of all; not that of only part of the population. In this light, becoming aware of historical contexts is important to move toward an inclusive society where everyone feels they belong and are wanted.

WHAT CAN ORGANIZATIONAL LEADERS DO?

By this point, you know that there is no running from the issue of religion in the workplace. Whether or not organizations have the deliberate goal of having a religiously diverse workplace, the reality is here. Religious and other forms of diversity will continue to increase and create more complex workplaces. We know now that creating an inclusive organization in the midst of religious diversity is possible—and that it requires the commitment of organizational leaders.

To that end, Deloitte, a leading consulting firm in the U.S., has generally identified six traits of inclusive leaders that we can apply specifically to religious inclusion (Bourke & Dillon, 2016):

1. Commitment. A leader must have a personal commitment to inclusion that draws both on their personal values and their belief in the business case for inclusion. When it comes to religious inclusion, that can mean finding common values between your beliefs and another's (for example, some version of The Golden Rule appears in many religious doctrines). It also means taking seriously the business case for religious inclusion, which we explored in Chapter 1.

2. Courage. Leaders must be courageous in speaking up for the inclusion of religion and religious people at work, bravely stepping up to advocate for others as they would themselves. Remember the case of Hamdi Ulukaya, the founder and owner of Chobani, who used his platform to both hire refugees, Muslim and not, and speak up for their inclusion.
3. Cognizance. At the same time, leaders must acknowledge their own biases and limitations. It's not a single leader's job to understand everything there is to know about religion, but rather to be curious and open about religion at work. Furthermore, cognizance entails harnessing a desire for fairness, so everyone is playing on the same field.
4. Curiosity. Being open to other ways of seeing the world is imperative to the inclusive leader. They also must be able to cope with ambiguity, embracing the reality that they can't know everything and thus will be faced with situations that require changing their mind. You'll remember that in Chapter 5 we discussed cultural models when exploring the clash between women who wear the hijab and American culture. Cultural models, or if you'd prefer mental models, are developed through our life experiences, drawing all the way back to how someone is raised. These deeply held and rarely examined beliefs about the way the world does and should work have a major impact on cultural settings such as the workplace. If we want to transform workplaces to become more inclusive of religious people, individual people have to be willing to change their own mental models.
5. Cultural intelligence. Curiosity naturally leads to cultural intelligence, as leaders who want to know more about others' religious identities will make sure to infuse this new knowledge into their everyday efforts and allow it to drive them forward as advocates for inclusion.
6. Collaboration. Collaborative leaders understand that we can do more together than we can apart. In other words, they know that diverse teams harness the power, voice, and insights of their members to become something more than any one individual could be on their own.

Of course, none of these leadership qualities exists in a vacuum. They are mutually reinforcing aspects of a leader that lead to inclusion-forward organizations. And, in fact, it's rare for an employee to attribute positive experiences at work to any one of these attributes, but rather to express gratitude for the employer. For instance, in my dissertation research explored at length in Chapter 5, one Muslim woman who wears the hijab reported having a very positive experience at work. "My employer is very understanding and flexible. My job even makes an exception for me to alter the uniform to best fit my modesty standards." Was this inclusive effort made because her employer was curious? Was it because management was courageous or culturally intelligent? Who knows? It doesn't matter. What matters is that this leader found a way to be responsive to and inclusive of the real human being standing before them.

If you don't see yourself as having all these qualities, don't worry! These aren't traits you're born with or without and it's likely rare for any leader to be perfectly proficient in all six categories. Rather than thinking of these as fixed items on a checklist, think of them as muscles that can be developed and strengthened—even for those who may feel they're already strong in any of the areas. For instance, to become more curious, you could keep a journal and write about how your own religious identity (or nonreligious identity) shows up at work. As you gather your thoughts on this, you could use the following prompts to ask yourself:

- Is this how you want to be included as a whole person?
- If you are included, are people from other religious identities treated likewise or is it only the dominant religious group?
- If they aren't included, who could you get to know to better understand the challenges they face?

This is one example of how you can change your mindset. If you'd like to learn more, I highly recommend reading Stanford researcher and psychologist Carol S. Dweck's book *Mindset: The New Psychology of Success* (2007). In it, she explores how we develop open mindsets so that we can embrace and be a part of an ever-changing world.

To further shift your organization to becoming more religiously inclusive, revisit the lessons we've drawn out in Chapters 5 through 9, from acknowledging cultural models to exploring the impact of religious freedom laws on the workplace. One of the best places to start is with the gap analysis framework I highlighted in Chapter 7. This process can be broken down into a handful of steps that will require time and effort—and can yield transformational results, so make sure to revisit that chapter where I discuss some of the forms these various steps can take and why they matter.

I want to take a moment to reiterate how important it is to have clearly and carefully written policies that reasonably accommodate all religious beliefs. Globally, most companies seem not to have formal, written policies on how to handle religion in the workplace. It is still an area that is largely left to discretion. However, real-life cases explored in this book and elsewhere have shown that having formal policies that articulate how to handle issues of religion and religious beliefs and practices may not be enough to create a religiously inclusive organization. A total commitment of the organization's leadership is also a necessity for success in this area. So is effective communication of the organization's policies aimed at fostering religious inclusion.

The next step is getting the whole leadership team on board—you might hand them this book or share any of the numerous resources we've cited to get them started. Regardless of what your leadership is engaged with, religious diversity and inclusion issues should be a C-Suite priority especially after the COVID-19 pandemic that began in 2019 and continues through the writing of this book.

This pandemic, and the inequalities it has unearthed, has given organizations another chance to take issues of diversity and stigma more seriously. Initiatives include offering training programs to employees to promote understanding and accommodation of diverse religious beliefs and views, and asking employees to sign anti-discrimination policies and agreements. While having initiatives that promote religious diversity and make everyone feel inclusive is not enough, the mere existence of such initiatives creates the impression that the organization has the intention of taking religious diversity and inclusion seriously. Moving from intention to action, however, involves embracing a proactive and strategic stance.

To help your organization become proactive, you'll need to assess where your organization is, as we've discussed with the Kaizen HC Model for Religious Inclusion. I'd like to offer you another tool all organizations should strongly consider leveraging to gauge your organization's religious inclusion: the Religious Freedom and Business Foundation's Corporate Religious Equity, Diversity, and Inclusion (REDI) Index.

The REDI Index measures religious inclusion at Fortune 500 companies, including how religious inclusion is publicly acknowledged by the company on their websites and with ERGs, as well as their explicit efforts to share best practices around religious inclusion with other companies and the public. It was originally designed by gathering input from leaders of Fortune 500 companies who are committed to religious inclusion and focuses on the areas these leaders see as most important to their religious inclusion efforts. At the same time, the REDI Index is a benchmarking tool that can help companies objectively chart their progress from year to year.

The index is already being used to evaluate the religious inclusion of major companies in the Fortune 500 and has utility for organizations of all sizes. In 2021, the two top-scoring companies among the 200 largest companies in America were Intel and Texas Instruments. Both Intel and Texas Instruments are recognized in part because of their significant investment into incorporating religious diversity into their overall diversity and inclusion work. At Intel, in fact, six of the 33 ERGs (nearly 20%) are specifically faith or belief based.

For the first time in 2022, the REDI Index will gather self-reported data via a survey. Areas of inquiry include:

- Religion is featured on company's main diversity page.
- Company shares best practices with other organizations.
- Religion is clearly addressed in diversity training.
- Attentive to how religion impacts stakeholders.
- Clear procedures for reporting discrimination.

As we've shown at length in this manuscript, these are all critical matters for creating real religious inclusion and belonging at the workplace. Even if you choose not to participate in the REDI Index, you can use the questions the Religious Freedom and Business Foundation has identified to help you develop and follow a strategic plan for religious inclusion.

Together the REDI Index, the Kaizen HC Model, and the SOAR framework can help any organization assess, evaluate, and chart a new path for religious inclusion and belonging.

WHAT CAN RESEARCHERS, STUDENTS, AND ACADEMICIANS DO?

Researchers, students, and academicians can use our unique skills to help organizations and policymakers understand the nuances of religious diversity and inclusion. Not only are there tensions between major groups of religions, there are also tensions inside these groups. Studies of intra-community disagreements and conflict at work could add much to the body of research, as could in-depth studies of major religious groups. As my research on women who wear the hijab demonstrates, intersectional explorations of religious inclusion can bring further nuance to the conversation as well.

WHAT CAN WE ALL DO?

The reality is that diversity is already a fact. We live in diverse societies and work in increasingly diverse workplaces. It's our job to make inclusion and belonging just as real.

The number one thing we can all do right now to make our workplaces and our worlds more inclusive is to become an ally. An ally is someone who is not from a marginalized group who fights for that group's rights and equality and advocates for their well-being. In her 2018 Ted Talk, writer Melinda Epler defined allyship as "understanding the imbalance in opportunity and working to change it." In other words, allyship is about seeing the ways society has limited the experiences and opportunities of some and the role we each have to play in changing society. Allyship is absolutely key for inclusion to be successful.

In her talk, Epler identifies three ways we can be better allies in the workplace. Here's how I see those playing out when it comes to workplace religious diversity and inclusion:

1. Do no harm. It's the job of allies to know how others are shut down and dismissed in the workplace and to not engage in those behaviors. For instance, if your organization only has social events with alcohol at them and provides no alcohol-free alternatives, speak up and request alcohol-free options for your Muslim, Jain, Buddhist, and Sikh colleagues—even if you won't drink them yourself.
2. Advocate for underrepresented people in small ways. When bias is confronted, whether intentional or not, behaviors change. So, if

your Muslim colleague who wears the hijab is constantly interrupted when she speaks, you can use your privilege to help her voice be heard. You can say something like "Sara was speaking and I'd like to hear what she has to say." It's a small effort, and it shows Sara she's not alone in the workplace and calls to attention the negative behavior.

3. Change someone's life significantly. Think of a time in your life that someone believed in you, took a risk on you, or encouraged you to go for a big promotion. You have the opportunity to be that person for someone else. Invest in your religiously diverse employees and colleagues like you would want someone to invest in you.

Governments and societies change because *people* change. If you want to see the world become a better place for all people inclusive of their religious identities, we have to start now. The work starts with you.

We hope this book and the stories contained within it have helped you both gain awareness of the need for religious inclusion and belonging and formed the foundation for you to become radically compassionate. Imagine for a second what it would be like to be at work and have your manager verbally and physically harass you because of your faith. How humiliating and terrifying would it be to have your manager rip the covering from your head? Imagine the feeling of helplessness you would feel if you were seriously ill but your employer did not let you take time off for a traditional healing ritual?

Some of you may have experienced just such realities in the workplace. Some of you may have witnessed such exchanges. Others may have at one time been the people who weren't accepting and receptive to religious needs. My sincere hope is that no matter who you have been, you will become a fierce advocate for your colleagues' and your own right to express any or no religion, so that we can all be not just safer, but better, together.

References

Bourke, J., & Dillon, B. (2016, April 14). The six signature traits of inclusive leadership. *Deloitte Insights.* https://www2.deloitte.com/us/en/insights/topics/talent/six-signature-traits-of-inclusive-leadership.html

Diamont, J. (2019). Europe experienced a surge in government restrictions on religious activity over the last decade. *Pew Research Center.* https://www.pewresearch.org/fact-tank/2019/07/29/europe-experienced-a-surge-in-government-restrictions-on-religious-activity-over-the-last-decade/

Dweck, C. S. (2007). *Mindset: The new psychology of success: How we can learn to fulfill our potential.* Ballantine Books.

EEOC. (2021). Religion-based charges (Charges filed with EEOC) FY 1997–FY 2020. https://www.eeoc.gov/statistics/religion-based-charges-charges-filed-eeoc-fy-1997-fy-2020

Epler, M. (2018). 3 ways to be a better ally in the workplace. *TED.* https://www.youtube.com/watch?v=k12j-E1LsUU

Pew Research Center. (2015). *Muslims.* https://www.pewforum.org/2015/04/02/muslims/

INDEX

CPSIA information can be obtained
at www.ICGtesting.com
Printed in the USA
LVHW081354110922
728103LV00001B/3